A Cocktail of Pain and Pleasure

Lord Rama's Maiden Journey into the Woods

AF663512

About the Author :

Eeshaan Mahesh is known for his spiritual mythological novels in Hindi literature. Along with being a sensitive writer, he is a deep meditator. His quest for inner truth led him to many great masters and Himalayan sages who not only satiated his thirst for truth and wisdom but also graced him with treasures of lost Himalayan meditation techniques. He is continuously helping and guiding people in various ways.

His writing reflects the most aesthetic expression of his own feelings and divine standards of love and devotion. One feels the authenticity of every character and witnesses how the inner -subconscious layers of mind force the characters to act and react to the situations. The art of writing the inner dialogues is the unique skill of Eeshaan Mahesh which enables the reader to relate it directly to them. The hidden mystery of these unique characters unfolds itself and leave an impression on the heart.

A Cocktail of Pain and Pleasure

Lord Rama's Maiden Journey into the Woods

Eeshaan Mahesh

Delta Book World
New Delhi - 110002

© Author

First Published in 2019
ISBN : 978-93-85719-13-4

All rights reserved including the right to translate or to reproduce this book or parts thereof except brief passages for quotations in articles or critical reviews.

Published by **Abhishek Goel** on behalf of

Delta Book World
G-4, Prahlad House
4832/24, Ansari Road
New Delhi - 110 002 (India)

Ph. : 011-2328 8140, 2324 5799
E-mail : deltabookworld@gmail.com

Illustrations by binduartaura.blogspot.com
English Translation by Mr. V.N.Gupta

PRINTED IN INDIA

Dedicated to

my wife

Bindu Popli

binduartaura.blogspot.com

whose paintings are

a humble effort

to look

through the

mysterious world of nature.

Foreword

Life is a cocktail of pain and pleasure. Sometimes we taste the sweet fruit of joy but many times it is the bitter fruit of pain that punctuates our life. There is always a preponderance of pain over pleasure. It is only once in a blue moon there is a silver lining of glee in the midst of clouds.

I fully chime in with the immortal words of Thomas Hardy, a great novelist of his time, who once wrote: "Happiness is an occasional episode in the general drama of pain." Our laughter is not pure or chaste. It is alloyed with tears.

The novel "Vanvass", originally written in Hindi by Eeshaan Mahesh, is entitled "A cocktail of Pain and Pleasure" which is a true testimony of it. The novel is well punctuated with a large area of 'Pain' surrounded by the orchestra of 'Pleasure'.

The very first episode deals with Dashratha, the Crown Prince of Ayodhya and Shravan Kumar casts light upon the basic truth of life of pain and pleasure. As hunting has been a passion for the royal families, Dashratha is no exception to it. Once he goes out hunting. He is imbued with the gift of shooting his arrow at the mere sound. But there have been mistakes as no human being is perfect. So, when Dashratha hears the sound of water being drunk, he mistakes Shravan Kumar to be a wild animal and discharges his arrow that hits his target. But unluckily the target turns out to be Shravan Kumar who comes to the river to take water for his aged, blind, thirsty parents. Since the arrow is poisonous, his death is certain. Dashratha is directed by Shravan Kumar to take water for his parents and tell them the truth. When Dashratha does so, his blind parents give up their ghost. But before dying, Dashratha is cursed that he will also meet the same fate. It is all a matter of pain and suffering for Dashratha as well as for Shravan Kumar's parents. Thus Dashratha's pleasure to be derived from hunting changes into pain. He is filled with remorse for having committed sinful deed of unintentional killing of not only one person but three.

Time doesn't stand still. It keeps on moving. According to the cycle of the fate, where there is a pain, there is a pleasure as well. A waft of joy blows Crown Prince, Dashratha, becomes a popular and strong king of Ayodhya. Dashratha convenes the meeting of his confidant ministers to discuss what measures should be adopted to get all the four sons married. There is a ripple of joy everywhere. But the arrival of Vishwamitra who comes to take Rama with him to deal with demons converts the joyous and gay atmosphere into dismal and gloomy one. But when

Vishwamitra returns with Rama and Sita, it turns out to be a red letter day for the entire royal family.

But who doesn't know that joy has wings? It is not perennial but transient by nature.The unexpected arrival of Parshurama casts clouds of sorrow and fear. He is furious when he comes to know that Rama has dishonoured Lord Shiva by lifting his bow and breaking it into pieces. He is fastidious; his anger can't be pacified easily. He is the one who had once taken a vow to eliminate Kshatriyas from the earth. But Rama is successful in pacifying him by virtue of his sagacity and tactfulness.

Then comes the climax of sorrow and sufferings when Dashratha leaves his mortal coil on learning from Kaikeyi that she wants Rama to be exiled for fourteen years and Bharata to be the king of Ayodhya in place of Rama. There is a great setback to the most-awaited coronation of Rama. It is due to the vicious role of hunch-backed Manthara that the atmosphere of gaiety is transformed into the ethos of gloom and disgust.

It has been rightly sat: "Melancholy has its shrine in the Temple of Delight."

V.N.Gupta

(Translator)

Reviews:

Eeshaan Mahesh's spiritual novels, based on Indian mythology have a mysterious flair. He speaks about those secrets which were never expressed before...

Ma Madhu
(Hrishikesh, INDIA)
Ma Madhu is the first disciple
of the Zen Master *OSHO*

After reading the first volume "Vanvaas" of the novel series Raghuvanshnatham by Osho lover Eeshaan Mahesh , we deeply felt that this is that 'Rama', Osho would have envisaged.

Eeshaan displayed such heights and depths of the character of the ruler, that he becomes the life force of his subjects. The more we read about Lord Rama, the more we realize that there is much more to discover and this is indeed the quality of such supreme souls. This book is a journey to know something more about them. We heartily wish and felicitate the author for writing such elated literature which gives flight to the hearts. This is all by God's grace and I am sure that the author is a blessed one.

------- Pandit Rajan- Sajan Mishra
(maestro of Indian Classical Music)
rajansajan@yahoo.com

I felt really pleased to read all six volumes of epic novel "Raghuvanshnatham" by Eeshaan Mahesh. The root concept on which the story stands strongly is how the ruler Lord Rama is constantly working to make a good, cultured and healthy society. He is determined to make his people happy and contented.

In all the creations the author has very skillfully allowed the reader to flow in its emotional sequences.

The character of Lord Rama which acts under a certain periphery has great depth and strength which the reader feels in all situations Rama encounters.

No doubt that the author has been blessed by the Divine Grace to express such unknown, unperceivable and mysterious incidents. My heartiest congratulations to Eeshaan Mahesh for his wonderful writing skills.

Dr. Beloo Mehra
beloome@gmail.com

The only paragraph that I can offer about your spiritual writings, and after knowing you for decades, is as following: Eeshaan Mahesh's novels are not to prove you that either God exists or that he is a knower of Him, but rather his writings drive you to the truth that you prove to yourself that you are the reality of Him.

Milovan Stankov
(Scientist & A Yogi from France)

1

Dashratha's joy knew no bounds today. The entire Kshatriya society was buzzing with the victory of the crown prince Dashratha. The royal family felt puffed up with pride at his skill of war strategy. Dashratha was an object of honour for many warriors, an object of jealousy for some and a symbol of idealism for his public.

The evening sky was overcast with rain-bearing clouds. It looked as if an army of clouds would eclipse the sky. Dashratha saw the clouds in different shapes of soldiers, horses, chariots, elephants, etc. Just then a whiff of cold, fast and fragrant air hit him and it was followed by a quick succession of wind carrying the smell of soil. The dusky clouds turned into black ones on account of their density. Hardly had the Sun peeped out of the clouds somewhere on the horizon when the waft of wind shut its doors. Suddenly there was a terrible flash of lightning in the midst of clouds. It wriggled as if tortured like a silver female serpent, and its tail's end touched the earth. A little later, Dashratha's arm fluttered as the sky's heart burst and it was followed by a terrible thunder. His hands were equipped with a bow. Closing his eyes, he lifted his face towards the sky. A thought came into his mind that since he had acquired

proficiency in the art of shooting a sound - piercing arrow, he should demonstrate it there and then itself after hearing the sound of planets-cum-constellations. He thought of making holes in the mighty bits of clouds which collided with each other and produced horrible sounds.

Dashratha's inner voice laughed sarcastically, 'Prince Dashratha is thinking of conquering nature by just gaining a little strength and proficiency in war- stategy. Hail to Prince Dashratha for his skill in the art of firing arrows at the sound!'

As soon as Dashratha heard this voice, the self-patronising wave stopped at once. He opened his eyes. The big drops of rain changed into torrential rain. In a short space of time there was water all around. One could hear the screams of peacocks. Every moment his desire was to target every word and destroy its source in this rain like peacocks, frogs, Jacobin cuckoo and even raindrops.

The sudden emergence of rain didn't give a chance to anyone to seek shelter. Even birds struggling with their wet feathers against severe strokes of wind were finding it extremely difficult to fly to trees. The cataracts falling from mountains were turning into white, red and ash colors as they were sweeping with them mountain metals, and were making a terrible noise.

At present, Dashratha's mind was like that of a mad elephant or of a young lion. He wanted to establish his rule over the entire nature. Violence was deepening in him. But how could he feel proud in killing innocent creatures? He wanted to hunt violent, dangerous ones like a violent wild buffalo, a mad elephant or a fiery- eyed lion.

His discretion spoke, 'Dashratha! It's Kshatriya's duty to control his power and discipline it. Power and pelf know only one thing, and it is to remove all hurdles and obstacles lying in their way like the speedy river falling from the mountain. They know only one type of dance, and it's only 'Tandava'- havoc. Only the good judgement can control and discipline these powers.'

'Hunting is Kshatriya's duty- his game, his practice,' Dashratha declared his decision to that voice. He climbed a gigantic tree very fast and murmured, 'There are many kinds of sounds in the rainy season. I'll identify the sound made by drinking animals and take their life by discharging my decisive arrows at them.'

While sitting on the branch of the tree, Dashratha was perplexed. He thought, 'What has happened today that no animal has felt thirsty. By this time many animals would have quenched their thirst at the Sarayu and I would have also pacified my instinct of hunting. But it seems that someone has today announced among the animals that Dashratha is sitting on the branch of a tree and is waiting for an animal to come to drink water so that he may kill it with his arrows.'

' Dashratha! Neither nature has anything to do with you nor anyone has announced among these animals about you lying in wait for them. But there is water everywhere on account of rainfall. So why should any animal come to the river?' the discretionary sense in Dashratha laughed wildly. It said, ' Dashratha, you are intoxicated with power and you have forgotten your practical sense.'

There was darkness all around because of black clouds. But rain had almost stopped falling. Just then Dashratha heard some sound in water. He cast his looks towards that direction. The sound was getting clearer and clearer. He immediately pulled the string of his bow and put an arrow on it.

He closed his eyes and tried to identify the sound in water to know whether it was the sound of an animal drinking water. He concentrated his mind. Inspired by it, his wisdom told him that it was the sound of water being put in a pitcher.

'No, nobody can come to fill his pitcher with water in rains and mud. Think once again,' Dashratha didn't like the voice of his wisdom.

'If it's so, then it's the sound of an elephant drinking water- an elephant that is thirsty and intoxicated, the one that is pulling water through its trunk to drink, and playing with it also,' wisdom giggled.

'Yes, it's very true.' There was a sort of flash of lightning in Dashratha's closed eyes. He quickly took off the arrow from the string of his bow. Then he took out a more powerful and poisonous arrow from his quiver and pulled up the string of his bow hard. Dashratha's concentration was now focused on that sound. It appeared as if the remaining noise of the world had subsided completely.

Buduk...Buduk...was the sound of water. Before hearing the sound of sucking water third time, Dashratha's word-piercing arrow which looked like a serpent had advanced towards its target.

A heart- rending scream "Ma..." pierced the atmosphere, making it resound. That shriek like a poisonous arrow got stuck into Dashratha's heart.

'O God! What have I done? This is the human voice. Has my arrow targeted the guiltless?' Dashratha's heart was filled with repentance.

Dashratha's entire body quivered with the feeling of sin. He got down the tree speedily and reached the place wherefrom the terrible human sound tinged with pain and grief was coming.

It seemed as if the human body floundering in mud had seen Dashratha standing by him. It also knew that he was the very person who had assaulted him with his arrow.

"Mother...Father...Oh! Who are you, the cruel person? What wrong had I done to you? I am only an ascetic. Then why did you make a violent attack on me?" The wounded person spoke painfully, "Oh! My old, blind and thirsty parents must have been waiting for me. I eat only the forest food. I am simply an ascetic who is engaged in serving his parents. What benefit will anyone reap by killing me? No, it will be nothing but atrocity. Ha! Ma..."

Dashratha felt as if he had become a statue of stone, as if the entire Himalaya mountain had fallen upon his body and soul. He bent over the painful injured body.

"O you killer! You've killed not one but three innocent persons with your one arrow. O Senseless! O unrestrained person! What have you done? O Mother! Oh!"

The bow and arrow fell down from Dashratha's hand. He was filled with grief and self-condemnation. The ascetic was heading towards death, and his agony was poisoning Dashratha's blood. His disheveled long hair was muddy. There was a pitcher on one side and his body was lying in the pool of red blood and mud. He looked towards Dashratha. His yogic eyes seemed to be burning Dashratha to ashes. There were numberless questions in his eyes, and Dashratha had no answer to anyone.

"Pardon me, O ascetic! Pardon me!" Dashratha folded his hands. He fell on his knees before the ascetic and in his quivering voice he said, "Who are you, O ascetic?"

"Now what's the use of seeking my introduction?" The ascetic smiled mildly. His smile was tinged with terrible agony, "I am Shravanna Kumar. I live in a cottage nearby and serve my old and blind parents. They were thirsty and I had come here to take water for them. Here I am going to die and there they are thirsty and full of apprehensions.

They will be waiting for my return. What do they know that the only staff of their old age and the apple of their eyes is on the verge of death, and a violent human creature has hunted him."

"O ascetic! I'm not a violent creature, but Prince Dashratha. But unintentionally I've happened to commit an utmost sinful deed."

"O Raghukula's Would- be King! You don't know that you've done a great misdeed. Just as an uprooted tree can't be saved, similarly the death of my parents is now certain and definite." Shravanna shrieked out of extreme agony. Trying to overcome his boundless pain, he said, "O king! This track goes up to my father's ashrama. You go there and quench their thirst. Tell them the whole truth. If you want God not to burn you with His curse, go and accept your guilt before my parents. Don't let them die in doubt."

Dashratha lifted the pitcher. No sooner did he turn, as if in a trance, than Shravanna Kumar raised his voice, "O king! Before going, pull out this arrow from my body. It's giving me intense pain like the one when the flooded river water devastates a sand dune."

"If I do so, you will immediately die and I'll hold myself responsible for killing a brahmin. Even otherwise I'am down with the guilt of a brahamin's death." Spoke Dashratha in his trembling voice.

"I am an ascetic, not a brahmin. My father is a Vaishya and my mother, a shudra. So, don't think you're a killer of Brahmin. I just want you to liberate me from this agony."

Dashratha knew that if his poisonous arrow could put even a huge- bodied elephant into a wretched condition, he was only an ordinary ascetic and how much agony he might be suffering from, he couldn't even think of in his imagination. Dashratha bent and took Shravanna Kumar in his lap. He held his shoulder with his left hand and pulled out his arrow with his right hand. Immediately, blood shot out in many streams. Shravanna Kumar looked towards Dashratha. There were many questions in his eyes. There were also signs of pain and fear in them. Blood came out from his mouth and with the last sound, his eyes became lifeless.

Dashratha was now trembling from head to toe. It started drizzling also. He filled the pitcher with the water from the Saryu River and stepped towards the track.

× × × ×

The track ended at a small wooden gate. In order to check the wild animals from entering, there were acacia trees and many thorny bushes surrounding the gate. There was an ordinary cottage in the middle. As the gate was pushed, there was metallic sound of things suspending from the gate. There were also bells used around the bullocks' neck.

"Shravanna, my son, you've come!" came from within the old woman's voice.

"Why did you take so much time in this terrible rainfall, Son? Your mother's heart is full of mysterious apprehensions." There was perplexity in the old woman's voice.

Dashratha got into the cottage.

"Shravanna!" called the old woman.

Dashratha's face turned white. When he saw the old, helpless, blind couple, Shravanna Kumar's words echoed in his ears- "O killer! You've killed three innocent persons. It's certain that soft- hearted parents of mine will breathe their last when they hear that you've killed their son."

"Son, why are you silent?" spoke the old woman. "We always disturb you. If you don't like any of the things of ours, don't bear it in your heart, son, with ill feeling. We feel gratified to be blessed with an austere son like you. You're the spark of our life, Shravanna! Our eyes, our life- everything you're for us. Say something, son!"

"Great Soul! I'm not your son. I'm Dashratha, a kshatriya," Dashratha's voice was quivering.

"It seems that you've lost your way and want to seek shelter." There was motherly love in the old woman's voice, "Son, call Shravanna who was on the bank of the Sarayu river. My son has gone to the river to take water. It seems that he's sporting in the holy water of the Sarayu river. Just bring him here. He'll welcome you."

Dashratha was over-brimmed with self-hatred. He felt as if he were a dirty gutter of sinful deed. Dashratha burst into tears, "Pardon me. I'm your culprit, a sinner." The old blind couple felt stunned. They kept listening to him.

Dashratha told everything to them. He kept looking at them without batting his eyelashes as he wanted to know their reaction. His sense of guilt made him feel that he was a poor wretch. When he killed many of his enemies and demons in wars, he felt puffed up with joy and pride. But now his one killing had stigmatised him.

The old man said, "Kshatriya! You've stood by truth. You didn't run away after killing my austere, innocent son. You're definitely prone to religion. That's why you came here and told us about your sinful deed though it was done unknowingly. If you had wished, you could have run away quietly. Then we could have breathed our last out of grief and ignorance, in wait for our son. But then do you know what would have happened? Your entire dynasty could have been destroyed by our curse. Destiny would never have pardoned you."

Dashratha thought for the first time why he didn't run away. People generally do so in this world. They try to hide their sin. And that place was absolutely desolate and lonely. Dashratha bowed his head before God within himself, 'O God! It's very kind of you that you didn't sow the seeds in me of running away after committing sinful deed; otherwise my mind would have been torn into pieces under the strain of sin- consciousness. It was I who didn't listen to You; You had alerted me every moment.'

"Take us to the place where our son's dead body is lying. We want to touch him- the one who was the only staff our old age," the old man's lifeless voice rose.

Dashratha took them to Shravanna Kumar's corpse. Some leaves from the trees had fallen upon it. Everything nearby was stained with red blood. The place where the arrow had been pulled out had turned into a deep pit. The blood and flesh lying there looked to be like burning hot coals. There was a strange kind of peace and a ripple of joy on his face, and its shineness seemed to be exclaiming, 'what a glorious deed of yours, O God!'

Both of them proceeded slowly towards their son's dead body, touched it gently and then they burst into wild sobs. "Our dear son! There was a time when you used to greet us when you met us, and today why aren't you speaking? Why are you sleeping on the ground in anger? Of course, I did sometimes use harsh words for you, so you may not speak to me. But your mother loves you intensely. Why don't you cling to her? Oh, son! If you don't converse with us, who will tell us stories from Scriptures and Puranas? Eh, Yamaraja! (The God of death) Set free my son!"

When Dashratha heard the woeful cry of the poor, helpless and blind couple, he felt as if nobody in this world was so mean and base as he.

"Our beloved austere son! You always served us at the cost of your own comforts and pleasures of life. May your soul be rest in peace!" The old man turned his face towards Dashratha, "O Kshatriya! O the Brave, the victorious and the Best Man!"

"Order me, great souls!" There was self- condemnation in Dashratha's voice.

"Now you end the game of our life also. Shoot your arrows upon us and send us with our son on the last journey of life."

"Have pity on us!" Dashratha was grief-stricken. "We're the objects of your mercy. Have pity on us also." It was the old man's explosive voice, "You Dashratha! We curse you. Just as we are found in this horrible, miserable, deplorable condition because of our son's death, you'll also find yourself in the same plight. You will leave your mortal coil in woeful tears and agony." The old man turned towards his wife, "you too hurl your curse upon this sinner."

As she touched her son's body, she was like a bird whose wings had been clipped. She fell upon her son's body. The old man did his best to excite her but it seemed she had already breathed her last.

"Ha, son! Ha, my austere Shravanna Kumar! Ha, son!" The scream of the old man seemed to have stopped the Sarayu river flowing.

Dashratha noticed that in his efforts to rise up, the old man like a drunken man fell upon his son's dead body and became still.

Dashratha bent upon his knees and fell upon the mud. He lifted both of his hands and face towards the sky, "O Destiny! Was I to be made the medium of this sinful deed? And is this a punishment for me? I am an unmarried prince. This punishment is nothing for me. Punish me, O Destiny!"

'Dashratha! The entire life lies before you for lamentation. Make amends for it also. But now you should perform the funeral rites of these people,' instructed Dashratha's sense of wisdom.

× × × ×

Dashratha woke up from sleep. His aged body was quivering with fear and weakness. He opened his eyes fully and turned them around the palace. He murmured," Why did the event that occurred twenty years ago appear in his dream as it is?"

'Dashratha, it's because of your diseased mind, ' laughed wisdom. 'You haven't slept well for the past so many nights. Work and fatigue have weakened your muscles. That's why you suffer from fear even in your subconscious mind while sleeping.'

'What should I do?' Dashratha passed his hand over his chest.

'Take energy- providing medicine from the physician and take rest or keep yourself busy. Get lost completely in pleasures of life, ' smiled wisdom.

At the motion of Dashratha, the gate-keeper came before him.

"Arrange the things at once for our departure. Tell the charioteer to hitch the horses. We have to go to the assembly as soon as possible." Dashratha got down from the bed, saluted the earth and gave the remaining instructions to the gate keeper.

* * *

2

All the required persons had already reached the assembly. This advisory body was neither political nor administrative but concerned with family matters. Therefore only very important ministers and royal priests had been invited to it.

Suyagya, Jabali, Kashyapa, Gautam, Markandey and Katyayan were sitting with Guru Vasishtha and Vamadeva. Among the ministers, Dhrashti, Jayanta, Vijaya, Surashtra, Rashtravardhan, Aakosh and Dharampala were sitting with Sumantra in front of them.

"Sumantra! Is the king well?" asked Vasishtha. "This is the first time when the king is absent without any prior information."

Before Sumantra said anything about it, Dashratha entered the assembly hall. Dashratha greeted Guru Vasishtha and acknowledged the greetings of ministers.

"Hon'ble Guru! Now it seems that I'm growing old physically." Dashratha folded his hands and said this smilingly to Vasishtha.

"O king! Only the mirror might have told you so." Vasishtha laughed and then there was a flash of joy on everyone's face.

" Hon'ble Guru, it's not the mirror but sleep has told so. Now sleep has begun to control my body." Dashratha explained to them why he got late by means of his helplessness.

"But it's the sign of young people, O king! You are again getting young because sleep overpowers only the young. The old don't get sleep. Congratulations to you on growing young again!" When Vasishtha laughed, all laughed. Dashratha himself couldn't help but laugh. Dashratha never prevented anyone from expressing his feelings and thoughts. Healthy thoughts and healthy jokes had always their legitimate places in his assembly. And their flow gained momentum when Dashratha's meeting was personal and connected with family, not administrative. There were hardly any restrictions or impositions of discipline of the state in that assembly.

"Then we'll discuss princes' wedding later. Let's first find out a suitable bride for youthful Dashratha," said Vamadeva comically.

Dashratha's face flushed. He came to the topic, "My Revered Gurus and Cordial members of the Cabinet! You all have been the source of Dashratha's voice, wisdom, thoughts and strength. It's only because of your sinless, greedless and selfless true advice that Ayodhya's people are happy and prosperous. It's due to your benign influence that Ayodhya kingdom eclipses even the brightness of paradise. All are here truthful and truth-loving, non-violent and healthy. When I see these virtues in my people, I feel overjoyed. All the people have beautiful and grand houses to live in. It's all due to your far-sightedness and adoption of the policy of 'Pro Bono Publico'. They have ornaments, sumptuous food stuff in more than enough quantity, beautiful and precious clothes. The water of rivers and tanks is sweet and energetic. There is no kind of ailment and sorrow. Ayodhya has been far away from the evil incidents of gambling, thefts, kidnappings and prostitution."

Dashratha rose from his seat and added, "And this is the outcome of all your untiring and matchless efforts." Dashratha folded his hands and touched his forehead with them in front of all present and spoke emotionally, "It's all the result of your blessings that I have four handsome sons who love one another and take care of the subject. They all have good conduct and behaviour. Even if a single prince walks upon the wrong path of life, the kingdom becomes the victim of misfortunes.

"Maharaja!" Sumantra folded his hands and said very humbly, "Like king, like subject! You are an ideal model for the masses. People see no fault in you. Therefore O faultless king! O Caretaker of the people! This is all your greatness. It's truly written in the scriptures that if a king is ethical, his subject will also be religion-bound. Now we wish you to say what lies buried in your heart. We'll try our best to implement it."

"Speak, O king!" Guru Vasishtha motioned Sumantra to sit down.

"Great guru! My ardent desire is to start looking for the brides for Rama, Lakshmana, Bharata and Shatrughana," said Dashratha. He added, "Even if the wedding of Lakshamana, Bharata and Shatrughana takes some more time, it doesn't matter. But Rama is the eldest. Therefore, if his marriage takes place as early as possible, I'll be free from a great responsibility. After that, I'll discharge other responsibilities."

"You're thinking in right direction, O king!" Vasishtha said, "Therein lies the rise and prosperity of Ayodhya."

"Then you yourself tell me how to proceed."

"We'll send marriage proposals to all those kingdoms which we think are suitable for us. We can send our state messengers also."

"I think Shri Rama's wedding should materialize at the earliest," said Sumantra.

"I too want the same thing, Sumantra! But I see a spark of suspicion in what you are saying. Am I right in thinking so?"

"You are right, Maharaja!" Sumantra bowed his head. He kept quiet for a little while. He cast his looks upon everyone and said, "These days whatever Rama is discussing or thinking is not in tune with Kshatriyas but mendicants. I guess from my talks with him that Rama is in turmoil of renunciation, and he wants to go to the forest, after renouncing everything here."

Dashratha looked at Sumantra seriously. He knew that Sumantra was not joking. Sumantra was such a sharp minister that he could see though what was going on in the mind of the other person. It seemed as if he were blessed with some divine knowledge.

"Sumantra!" There was a trace of worry in Dashratha's voice, "Is Rama dissatisfied with us or any policy of ours?"

"No, never Maharja!" Sumantra was able to see through Dashratha's anxiety, "Rama is par excellence. I've probed his mind deeply. He knows no such word as discontentment. Maharaja! The truth is that if heaven is lusterless in comparison to Ayodhya, it's not because of us or you, but because of Shri Rama's sensitiveness, duty-consciousness and untiring labour.

"Sumantra is telling the truth, O king!" There was a touch of pride in Vasishtha's voice, "Sumantra has talked about Rama's renunciation. As a matter of fact, that is Rama's sensitivity. Rama is overbrimmed with numerous curiosities and he often shares them with me. It is certainly God's blessing; otherwise princes in the initial stage of their youth are often found plunged in seeking worldly pleasures of life and hunting wild animals. But Rama and his remaining brothers aren't at all vain of being princes. When I see the princes of other kings of the country, they are often intoxicated with royal power. They wander about here and there, troubling their people like a wild buffalo. They order their bodyguards and soldiers to force their power upon the common masses."

"But, Maharaja!" Sumantra wiped his tearful eyes, "Though Rama age-wise has just entered the prime youth of his life - a mere adolescent- yet the people look upon him as their father. They say that Rama always takes care of us as a mother does of her child. Rama along with Laksmana moves about among the people all the time. They see whether the state department is doing its assigned work and serving the people in the right direction or not. When Rama, being a prince, started doing like this, some corrupt officials thought that the prince would do so only for a few days and then return to his palace. But Rama told the lazy and indifferent corrupt officials angrily that he would never tolerate indiscipline and their corrupt conduct.

Its result is that now all the departments work faithfully. Whatever money is given to them by the state for the development of the people is now spent on them. If I tell you, Maharja! What I've in my mind," wiping his joyous tears, "it seems to me that Rama is the incarnation of God. He is such a sea of mercy, pity, egalitarianism and sympathy that he can only be God. These virtues aren't human. It seems that whatever words of glory have the

Vedas expressed for God, they are all for Rama. Rama can be compared only with Rama. Rama is matchless."

Dashratha was full of joy, happiness and pride. He thought of leaving his place to take Sumantra in his arms, but he hesitated to do so.

Vasishtha looked at Sumantra smilingly and raised his hand as if to bless him. Sumantra bowed his head.

"Victory to Maharaja!' entered the gate-keeper and stood with his bowed head.

"O Gate-keeper!" There was a tinge of command in Dashratha's voice, "Orders had been issued that he must not be disturbed while he was in a very important council. Then what befell at the main gate because of which you were sent here in the midst of our meeting?"

"Maharaja! Vishwamitra, Gaadhi's son, of Kushik dynasty, has honoured us with his presence, and he wants to meet you just now," the gate-keeper again bowed his head.

On hearing the name 'Vishwamitra', all were greatly amazed and they all looked at one another in surprise.

"Ayodhya is fortunate enough to be visited by the great Rishi Vishwamitra." Dashratha's face kindled with joy, "He had been in meditation for a long period of time. The whole world longed to meet Vishwamitra so that their countries might feel gratified by his arrival. The land where Vishwamitra has himself arrived is fortunate."

"Brahmrishi Vishwamitra! From a Kshatriya to Brahmrishi nobody has ever undertaken this journey. Nobody else can be likened to the great scientist, Vishwamitra who is the inventor of different kinds of weapons and arms. Vishwamitra thinks of the welfare of the entire earth," Vasishtha's voice conveyed his feeling of respect for him.

"But, O Great Rishi! We do know that there are differences between you and the great sage," Vijay, the minister smiled.

"Vijay!" Vasishtha too smiled, "But it doesn't mean that we should not acknowledge the great qualities of any man or the one who belongs to the opposite faction. We aren't supposed to be indifferent to them."

Dashratha looked at Guru Vasishtha devotionally and began to think, 'How lucky I am to have such a great guru for his sons! Vasishtha himself is free from the maladies of jealousy, envy and vanity. He's a guru who has a wholesome mind. That's why his presence has enriched Rama, Lakshamana, Bharata and Shatrughana with good conduct.'

Guru Vasishtha stood up to go to welcome Vishwamitra. Dashratha and others moved towards the special guest-house.

Dashratha saw that Vishwamitra's visage was shining brightly with divine glory like the Sun. He was feeling the divine energy within him. According to the scriptural methods, Vishwamitra's feet were washed and adorned with flowers.

"May God bless you with fame!" Vishwamitra raised his hand as if to bless Dashratha and looked at him affectionately.

Dashratha shrank from within like a beggar who has got less than what he expected. It was like a trifle alms given by a person like Vishwamitra who was a great king-like. Vishwamitra was a great ascetic who had boundless divine power. He knew whatever blessings he gave would certainly be fruitful. But 'May God bless you with fame!' was nothing but an insignificant blessing, thought Dashratha. He was not a poet, a dancer, a painter, a sculptor or a singer who longed for fame. He is a king, and kings like the blessings of an increase in power and pelf.

"O King!" There was limitless patience and depth in Vishwamitra's voice, "I am contented to know that the people of your kingdom are not only leading a comfortable but also a happy life. If the people are good charactered and well-cultured, the whole tribute goes to the king only. In my perspective, nowhere else do I find the people of any kingdom so happy as yours are. Your people praise you from behind your back and pray for your welfare. Gentle king! Gentle!"

Brahmrishi Vishwamitra was the one who was never contented with anything, for whom discontentment and insatiety were the sources of his power of austerity. He believed that there should be a flame of deep discontentment rising in one's heart to achieve something in life, to be pushed towards one's goal. But what a wonderful discontentment of his! This is what we call 'Satvik Discontentment'- where there is no desperation, no agony, only thirst - the thirst to make humanity happy. That's why he never misused his powers despite the fact that he was the inventor of weapons. After becoming the Brahmarishi, his soul roamed only in 'Brahma'. And this very Vishwamitra was so happy with Dashratha's administrative set up! Feeling extremely happy, Dashratha bowed his head once again before Vishwamitra and said in his trembling voice, "It's all due to the blessings of Brahmrishi who is so happy with his servant."

"Dashratha! It's hoped that the enemies on the boundary line of your kingdom will be under your control. And if any enemy raises his head against you, you can discipline him." There was a spark of his blessings in Vishwamitra's voice.

"The Great Guru Vasishtha!" There was happiness on Vishwamitra's face.

"Then I'll also have to call you Brahmrishi Vishwamitra," Vasishtha laughed wildly.

"Do you want to boost my vanity by calling me a brahmrishi?" giggled Vishwamitra also. "These titles simply go to augment our false pride and arrogance."

"Yes, if anyone remains stuck to them." Vashishta's voice was somewhat philosophical, "A man finds himself intoxicated with his title out of ignorance. He begins to think that nobody has an existence before him."

"Every title should be like a fruit's skin. After eating the fruit of knowledge and digesting it into blood, one should forget the title." Vishwamitra heaved a sigh, "When consciousness develops its wings and it begins to sail in the far-off sky, it realises how mean and little the evils of mind are, when it is in the weightless state. Humanity should also catch its flight. The motto of all rishis is: 'Pro bono publico'."

The entire group of priests and counsellors was full of devotional joy, standing before Vishwamitra. They were concentratedly bearing in their heart each and every word of Vishwamitra.

Vishwamitra's eyes fell upon Dashratha. He noticed that Dashratha was mentally lost in some other world. He seemed to have lost in his dream. All others also looked at Dashratha, and Dashratha was unconscious of it.

"Maharaja!" Sumantra called him just to bring him out of his dream.

Dashratha woke up from his dream in haste and hesitated a little.

"What were you thinking, O king?" Vishwamitra asked him casually.

"Great Soul!" Dashratha's voice was joyful, "This time I was feeling like a man advancing towards his old age as if he had got nectar to drink, as if the drought-hit area had got torrential rainfall. Just as I was besides with joy when I was blessed with sons after so many years of being childless, in the same way, I'm feeling extremely happy. And you are the cause of all this treasure. Your arrival has made me feel like that beggar who had been gifted with wealth by Kuber, the treasurer of wealth. Brahmana! My life has become meaningful, I feel gratified. Cordially I want to serve you and feel lucky. You always wander in Brahmlok itself and so you are a living image of Brahma. It seems from your arrival that pilgrimage itself has come to my house and I've got the fruits of many pilgrimages while sitting at home. Speak out, my lord, what's the motto of your arrival here? I'm ready to serve you like a servant whatever you deem fit for me." There were tears of joy in Dashratha's eyes.

Vishwamitra said nothing. He kept on looking at Dashratha with his silent eyes. Then he cast his looks upon all others, and then once again his looks settled down upon Dashratha. He smiled gently. It looked as if he were going to say something. But he remained silent.

"Maharishi!" said Dashratha in his gentle voice, "Don't hesitate at all. Don't give room to any such idea whether I'll be able to serve you or not. I'll feel gratified if I am able to fulfill your desires."

Dashratha once again looked at Vishwamitra's face like a supplicant to know what was going on in his mind. All others were also waiting for Vishwamitra to say something.

"Dashratha!" Vishwamitra said calmly, "On this earth you're like a lion among the present kings. I don't find elsewhere the feeling which you have for religion and duty. The generous words which you have just uttered are in tune with your nature; and why shouldn't it be so? The king who has a royal guru like Vasishtha is like a rishi in his deportment. Why are other kings cruel and wisdomless? It's because they have state gurus who chime in with them. They don't lead the king to the path of truth. This is the greatest problem before a king that if he has started walking upon the wrong path, there's nobody to make him realize his mistakes. Generally, nobody dares go against the wishes of the king out of fear and greed. But the state guru is that power which can keep the king in discipline. You always follow the path of truth under the guidance of Vasishtha; so I want to tell you the purpose of my visit to you. I am confident that truth-bound Dashratha will do my work."

A suspicion arouse in Dashratha's mind. Before uttering the purpose of his visit, why did Vishwamitra say, 'the truth-bound Dashratha will do my work.' After all, what is it that Vishwamitra is going to ask him to do? And why had he to bind Dashratha to his word? After becoming a brahmarshi he was leading his life like a solitary scientist in his chaste ashrama. The world had forgotten that he went anywhere else. He was all the time busy performing yajnas in the world of divine powers. He is the one who has bidden good-bye to all his desires and ambitions. Then what is it that brought him to Dashratha with a special motto?

"O, Superior of men!" Vishwamitra seemed to be lost, "I 'm making an experiment. If I perform any religious rite for its success, demons come and destroy it. They kill the co-performers of yajna and celibate persons mercilessly. Now it has come to such a pass that my ashram dwellers have started thinking of going elsewhere out of fear."

"But you're full-fledged in adequacy, great rishi!" said Sumantra in his worried and surprised voice." There's nobody else so much adept in valour and knowledge of weaponry as you are."

"Sumantra! Fame and might don't always remain same for all times to come. When I was a Kshatriya, I was chivalrous and I proved it also. Now, according to the cycle of time, my physical strength has reduced and knowledge has strengthened." Vishwamitra was unfolding everything by and by, "A rishi who dwells in an ashrama is not a warrior. He doesn't leave outside the ashrama platoons of soldiers out of fear of violence. He can't check demons from making an assault. Even otherwise the nature or deed of ascetics, celibates, recluses, mendicants and sages is not to fight war. This is the responsibility of kshatriyas to quell evil persons and protect the weak."

"O Great Sage!"There was an element of surprise and glory in Dashratha's voice, "What benefit will the demons get from their attack on accomplished ashramas?"

"O King!"said Vasishtha, "The same what an enemy gets from his attack on a rich man."

"Wealth!" There was a streak of astonishment on Dashratha's forehead, "Where is so much wealth in any ashrama that becomes the centre of attraction for demons to attack?"

"O King!" smiled Vasishtha, "Wealth doesn't mean only gold or currency. Wealth means a valuable thing."

"I'm also saying the same thing, gurudeva, what priceless thing is found in an ashrama, which…"

"...the wealth of knowledge!" Vasishtha didn't let Dashratha complete his sentence. He looked towards Vishwamitra and said, "The great rishi is equipped with the knowledge of divine arms and weapons. He knows the devices of launching them. He is expert in making new arms. This is true that Vishwamitra is a great scientist and the demons want to make use of that science to destroy humanity."

"Say, the great rishi! What are your orders for me?" Now everything was quite clear to Dashratha. He knew what Vishwamitra wanted from him- some soldiers to protect his ashrama and some money for the arrangement of yajna. If he had sent this simple message to him, couldn't he have accomplished his wishes? Didn't he have that much faith in Dashratha? Anyhow, it's his grace upon him that he's visited his place.

"O King of Kings!" There was divinity in Vishwamitra's voice, "A major part of this great experiment of mine is accomplished. The last seven days are very important and critical. If at that time the powerful and educated demons like Mareech and Subahu cause blood-shed within my ashrama, a large part of this priceless yajna will become fruitless. So I want your truthful and chivalrous eldest son, Rama to give protection to this yajna."

"Rama!" Dashratha gasped in surprise and his eyes became lusterless and lifeless.

"Yes, Rama!" Vishwamitra said calmly, "Rama under my protection is capable of killing those demons by virtue of his chivalry and divinity. I'll make Rama competent enough in every way. After getting that divine power, your son, Rama will become renowned in the entire world. This will give momentum to your Raghukula's fame."

Dashratha said to himself grumblingly, 'It has been truly said that a man loses his natural sense of wisdom in his old age. He was himself saying a little while ago that he was no longer as brave as he used to be. Now he is saying that under his protection Rama will be able to kill those demons by dint of his valor and divinity. The person who can't protect himself and has come to the king to get aid from him is now saying that he will protect the one who protects him. What has happened to Vishwamitra? Are the people in this world beating their drums in praise of this Vishwamitra whose knowledge is impractical?

What a comical and childish demand that Rama who is only a child should be sent to fight demons and protect yajna! Vishwamitra himself was saying that fighting war was no longer a part of his nature. He doesn't understand the simple thing that war doesn't lie within the nature of children also.'

Vishwamitra saw the mental condition of Dashratha as if he felt undone, as if someone had bitten him to death. It was quite clear from the emotions which emerged on Dashratha's face that he was diving in a pool of wonderment.

"O king! It's quite but natural to be obsessed with the feeling of love for son, but you should forsake your love for son." Vishwamitra added, "Take it for granted that Rama has killed these demons."

But Dashratha's innermost feelings were poisoning his mind, 'This old Vishwamitra has become whacky. He says that we should suppose that Mareech and Subahu have been killed by Rama. He thinks that these two demons and their army are like flowers in a creeper and Rama goes there and plucks them.'

Dashratha felt the whip of his intelligence, 'A little while ago you were extremely happy. What was the need of talking tall? Why were you ready to do everything for this rishi? More than this, you have made 'Let life go, not the word' the hallmark of Raghukul ! Now you are stuck in your own spider's web. Dashratha, you might have heard a proverbial saying 'Bull come and kill me', you always do the same. Now bear it. This rishi is an obstinate person. He won't leave the place without Rama. And you also know that you'll have to send Rama with this incompetent, helpless recluse to maintain your decorum. How can he protect your son when he is incapable of protecting himself? When the demons come to know that Dashratha's eldest son Rama, a mere child, who has accomplished his education only recently and who is inexperienced, has come to fight them and punish them they'll first kill your Rama. It'll boost their terror. Other kings will also tremble with fear thinking that the demons that can kill even Dashratha's son will be very strong and powerful. Rama is just like a rabbit in the flock of these demons who are like wolves. They will tear Rama into pieces and chew him. Then this same rishi, after death, will preach you about philosophy and spiritualism. He'll say, 'O King! Destiny was against us. Whatever is to happen will happen. It can't be undone. Your son has died a heroic death; so don't be grief-stricken, O king...'

Dashratha felt choked in the smog of these thoughts. He found it difficult to breathe easily. He felt as if someone was throttling him and continuing to do so. The ground, chamber, sceptre and all the present persons seemed to be revolving before his eyes very fast. Dashratha held his forehead. As he was going to faint and fall, Sumantra standing by didn't let him do so. He helped him sit down on a seat and called out, "Maharaja! Maharaja!"

"Fetch water!" Vasishtha said seriously. There was a commotion among the remaining important persons.

The sprinkle of water on Dashratha's face made him open his eyes. He sipped a little water and tried to be his normal self. He was feeling ashamed of himself thinking what others would be feeling about him that Dashratha was so weak and fearful from within or that he showed signs of his ripe age. Dashratha controlled himself. He saw that his faint had no impact upon Vishwamitra. He was sitting quite confidently as before.

"Raghunandana!" Vishwamitra's voice was somewhat dry, "I have dearth of time. Instead of being worried or aggrieved, take permission from your councillors and Vasishtha, and order Rama to accompany me for ten days.

Vishwamitra's stubbornness put Dashratha into agony again. He thought that the rishi knew no decorum at all. When he became unconscious, instead of asking about his welfare, he put forward his selfishness before him. He wouldn't be able to understand the sufferings of soft-hearted Rama. Dashratha began to curse his fate from within, 'O Destiny! What game are you playing with me? I was thinking of Rama's wedding and you made a plan to send him into the jaws of death.'

'Dashratha! Tell this rishi that his decision is comical and far from far-sightedness. If he doesn't agree to it, offer him some temptation. But do something without late.' Dashratha's sense of wisdom pushed him into this context like a swimming coach who pushes his student into a swimming pool all of a sudden.

"Maharishi!" Dashratha sweetened his voice too much so that Vishwamitra might not suspect even a little bit that Dashratha within his heart of hearts was looking upon his arrival as an unhappy and inauspicious sign, "Rama is a mere boy of sixteen. We still take him to be so soft-hearted that we call him a lotus-eyed boy. The child Rama isn't competent enough to fight the demons. Even if you take Rama and your work doesn't accomplish, then what is its use? My large army consisting of many elephants, horses, chariots, etc. is world renowned for its chivalry. Under my command it will protect your yajna. Leave the idea of taking Rama with you. O Great Rishi! I myself take the responsibility of protecting you."

To know Vishwamitra's reaction, Dashratha paused. He felt that Vishwamitra would be affected by his logic and would realise that his motto was only to get protection for his yajna. He would think if Dashratha himself was desirous to go with him, what he would do with the boy Rama. Before Vishwamitra said anything, Dashratha himself spoke out, "O Great Sage!" He made his voice comical, an index that Vishwamitra's demand was childish, "Rama has accomplished his general education in deportment and weaponry recently. He can't gauge other people's strength. Nor has he any experience of war. Nor has he any knowledge of launching weapons. He isn't expert in warfare strategy like you."

"I'm not ignorant about this aspect." Vishwamitra looked at Dashratha as if with severe eyes, "I have full knowledge about Rama. I'm acquainted with each and everything of Rama. I've simply come here to get a direct proof of what I've heard of him. I want to see with my own eyes whether it is the same Rama whom I seek or he is only an ordinary prince of an ordinary king Dashratha and is immersed in luxuries of life like the other kings."

"O Great Sage!" Dashratha felt vexed from within, "You're not trying to understand the gravity of the situation. You know very well that the demons are the masters of illusory powers. They wage war by adopting different kinds of deceptive means. If you still insist on taking Rama with you, I'll also go with you accompanied by my large army. If there is any need of more army units, I'll arrange for that also. Please tell me more in detail about the enemy. I am supposed to know about the might of ones whom I've to face." Dashratha thought that when Vishwamitra told him about the strength of demons, he might himself feel that the deed for which Rama was required was not suitable for him. In such a state of affairs he would himself drop his impractical obstinacy.

After hearing Dashratha, Vishwamitra smiled.His deep and intense smile was telling Dashratha that he was able to read Dashratha's thoughts. He said, "You might have come to know about the demon Ravana who was born in Maharishi Pulastya's dynasty. The demon Ravana is the brother of Kuber, the master of wealth and the legitimate son of Vishrava sage. Boundless wealth and might have made him a demon. He has an unconquerable fort in the impenetrable island of Lanka. Protected by the chivalrous army, he lives in a palatial house in Lanka city which outbeats even Heaven in glory. From there itself he controls all his demoniac activities. He himself is plunged deeply in wine and women, but the demons appointed by him create the havoc on earth. All the kings in their own regions are at the mercy of Ravana. They have no courage to go against his wishes. They have accepted Ravana's suzerainty. This is the reason why these demons fearlessly indulge in their daily cruel deeds of murder, kidnapping and rape. When they see any sage or saint performing any yajna, they create terror there. There is a reign of terrorism and cruelty everywhere, Dashratha! Demoniac terrorism!"

Dashratha beat his forehead and wiggled inwardly, 'Are the divine knowledgeable persons stupid? This brahmrishi Vishwamitra doesn't know what he wants and what his demands are. His condition is like that of a child whose toy has been trampled upon by a soldier's horse's hoofs, and he goes to the village headman asking him to give him his son the toy so that he may kill the king's army.' Dashratha looked at all the present nobilities. They were all looking at Dashratha. They were sure that Guru Vasishtha could understand his mental condition.

"Maharishi! You deserve my respect. You're my guru, my god. Please have mercy upon my son and me, the unlucky Dashratha." There was a touch of politeness and humility in Dashratha's voice. He stood before him with his bowed head. But behind this meekness his feeling was the same as that of a courteous but embarrassed rich man before a beggar who says, 'Please go and visit some other house.'

"I've come to bless you. When I came here, you praised me in diverse ways and felt fortunate. Now all of a sudden how have you become unfortunate?" There was severity in Vishwamitra's voice.

"It's because, great sage, I can't face that evil-minded Ravana. In a war Ravana sucks his enemy's strength. Even gods, demons, yakshas, nagas, garuda and gandharvas can't bear his speed. Ravana is the living image of 'death'. Death itself salutes him. Then a simple man is insignificant before his valor. I along with my whole army and sons am incapable of fighting war with him."

"But when did I tell you to fight Ravana?" There was a comical smile tinged with strictness on Vishwamitra's face. He was shooting arrows of sarcasm at him, "Why are you reciting here a poem about Ravana's power and revealing your cowardice? Rama has to fight only Mareech and Subahu."

"Great Sage! You know that they're the sons of great demons like Sunda and Upsunda. At the time of battle these two are like the living images of Yamraja, the god of Death. They are adept in all sorts of warfare strategy. They're the two hands of Ravana in power and valor."

"O King!" Vishwamitra said in a sarcastic tone, "You relinquish your kingly duties and start writing a book on demon's strength, bravery, their warfare strategy and terror. You're competent enough to do so."

Vishwamitra was unveiling Dashratha's weakness in front of his priests and ministers. Dashratha was silent because he was supposed to live within his bounds and courtesy. But now he made up his mind to be somewhat severe. He said, "Great Soul! I'll not allow Rama to go with you."

"O King!" Vishwamitra's patience gave way. The lava within his heart was boiling before the volcano burst. It seemed it would burn Dashratha. He said furiously, "First, you make a promise and then you break it. You adorn yourself with the words that you will keep your word even at the cost of your life. If you think it to be right, I'll go as I came. And then you...you remain in the world of your false promises and false fame."

Vasishtha thought that the matter was going out of hands. If he didn't intervene at this juncture, Vishwamitra who came with the expectation of ending the terror caused by a few demons might return and determine to destroy the kingdom of Dashratha.

Vasishtha didn't let Vishwamitra say anything further. He turned towards Dashratha and said, "Maharaja! Brahmrishi is right what he says. You shouldn't relinquish your virtue. It's not in tune with your dynasty's fame and honour. Do you know one thing is very famous in all the three worlds? And it is that king Dashratha of Raghukula is an embodiment of virtues. It doesn't behove you to carry a bundle of sins on your back. If a king makes a promise that he shall do this work and doesn't do, his decline is certain. I, therefore, request you to send Rama with Vishwamitra ji."

Dashratha got stunned when he heard Vasishtha. He began to think, 'My condition is like that of a king whose own truthworthy army chief is stabbing him on his back. I was thinking Guru Vasishtha has got a golden chance to put his opponent Vishwamitra to shame for his foolishness, but here it seems that he himself is an accomplice of his conspiracy. After all, what's this all happening around me? Why don't these great rishis understand a simple thing which I do?

"Under the patronage of Vishwamitraji Rama is as safe and sound as a vase of nectar in the midst of terrible fire raging all around." Vasishtha looked at Vishwamitra and found that there was not a single mark of anger and severity on his face. It seemed that he was now quite confident of success of his mission. Vasishtha turned towards Dashratha, and said, "It is true Rama isn't so much skilled in weaponary and warfare strategy as to accomplish this task. But this is also true that nobody else is like Vishwamitraji who has a perfect knowledge of arms and weapons. Except me nobody else truly knows brahmrishi nor can anyone know him. Under his guidance Rama is completely safe. You shouldn't entertain any doubt about it. You may be thinking it as a matter of your bad luck. But O king! This is the time of the rise of the whole world, not only of yours. Rama can never get a better guru than Vishwamitra. From today itself the time has arrived for Rama to begin his practical training in warfare. Tomorrow when Rama becomes the king, how will he go to great wars without any experience in war? Whatever knowledge I have given him in launching weapons is simple and ordinary. But what Vishwamitrji gives to Rama, that will not only be extraordinary but also matchless. I have studied Rama deeply. O king! It's your good luck that Brahmrishi Vishwamitra himself has come here to become Rama's guru and give him divine training in war. You should, therefore, see off Rama happily."

Dashratha thought, 'It's true that nothing is there in man's hand. Despite my wish and knowing everything, I can't say 'No' to it. When guru Vasishtha is not my own, how can I expect my ministers and other councillors to support me? Now I must act in such a way as done earlier that it doesn't reveal my weakness at all."

"Great Rishi!" said Dashratha with happiness on his face and in his voice, "May you be happy, Brahmrishi! Whatever I said to you, "it was from a father's heart. Who doesn't know infatuation of a father for a son? If I am the king, it doesn't mean that I'm devoid of emotions and impulses. But I am conscious about my responsibilities, my promise and your word of bringing back Rama safe. I'm also under the influence of guru Vasishtha's advice and his far-sightedness. So now I hand over my eldest son Rama to you for safeguarding the yajna."

"May you be blessed with good-will and prosperity, O king!" Vishwamitra was quite contented and said, "I'll bring back Shri Rama to you after ten days."

Immediately Dashratha ordered to make arrangement for Rama's departure, and then sent for him.

× × ×

Rama came. Vishwamitra looked at Rama with his experienced eyes of a judge. He found Rama to be a lion among men. Rama was physically strong and stout. He was handsome. There was calmness and purity in his eyes. There was no trace of arrogance or ego in them. As Rama approached, he greeted them all in a proper way according to their rank.

"Give me orders, father!" Rama's voice was melodious and poetic. He said, "Which task of yours is dear to you? I would like to accomplish it by walking upon your path of truth, morality and religion."

Vishwamitra gazed at Rama with fascination. He realized that Rama's soul was quite sensitive to religion, faith and all limitations.

Dashratha apprised Rama of the whole situation. Rama turned towards Vishwamitra, "Gurudev! I am at your service. I've already heard the stories of your greatness from Guru Vasishtha. I am your devotee and bow my head in honour to your divine light."

Vishwamitra paid special attention to Rama's two statements. These two sentences created a ripple of joy in his heart. Instead of addressing Vishwamitra by such titles as 'Maharishi', 'Munishreshtha', 'Rishishreshtha', 'Brahmrishi' which only go to enhance one's ego, Rama honoured him with 'Gurudeva' which reflected his affiliation, his sense of belongingness and adoration for Vishwamitra. It also reflected his feeling of being a disciple of Vishwamitra. Another sentence of Rama that he was devoted to Vishwamitra on account of his divine light enchanted brahmrishi. The entire world honoured him with 'Brahmrishi' but Rama didn't do so.

'My son, Rama!" Vishwamitra's voice was overbrimmed with love for Rama ," Let's go."

"As you wish, Gurudev! But I have to make a request to you."

"Say, Rama! Without any hesitation!"

"I never hesitate in asking questions out of curiosity. Gurudev! You shouldn't think that if I put a question to you out of eagerness, it is disobedience on my part or my indifference to you," said Rama.

"Speak!"

"Lakshmana accompanies me in every situation. In other words, my soul resides in him. I'll feel gratified if you permit me to have Lakshmana with me," said Rama.

Vishwamitra looked at Lakshmana. Like terrible fire rising at the time of yajna, he was healthy and had pure redness on his face. Lakshmana was standing by Rama as if he were an integral part of Rama's body. Rama had already declared that Lakshmana was the fibre of his life. By way of giving his consent, Vishwamitra closed his eyes, bent his head, smiled affectionately and raised his palms as if to bless them.

3

Vishwamitra asked them to stop chariots at the main gate of Ayodhya. All chariots stopped moving.

"Rama! Now we'll walk on foot."

"Ji, Gurudeva!"

"Rama! What has happened?" asked Sumantra when he saw that Vishwamitra had stepped down from the chariot with Rama and Lakshmana.

Sumantra also alighted from his chariot and came to them to know its reason.

"Kaka!" There was a sense of affiliation to the utmost degree in Rama's voice. He said, "It's the wish of Gurudeva that we now walk on foot."

"Sumantra!"spoke Vishwamitra, "We i.e Rama, Lakshmana and I alone will proceed without any goods, any royal official or servant." It was quite clear from Vishwamitra's statement that it was his decision.

"But, great sage! It's the order of Maharaja Dashratha that..."

"Kaka! Gurudeva accepted Maharaja Dashratha's wish to a certain limit. Now you should cooperate with him in a matter of future plan. You're requested to obey gurudeva's wish as if it were the orders of Maharaja Dashratha."

When Vishwamitra heard such well-groomed, well-cultured and sweet decisive words of Rama, his affectionate honor for Rama arose in his heart. He wanted to step forward to embrace Rama and say, 'Rama! You're amazing. You don't get entangled with any obstacle rising in the way. Only that king is ethical who works for the welfare of common masses and overcomes every hindrance by virtue of his strong decision.'

Vishwamitra saw strength hidden in Rama's words. Sumantra immediately ordered all the officials concerned with the arrangement of state journey to return to Ayodhya. In other words, Sumantra knew very well that no change was possible in Rama's decision. So he gave no place to any logicality like Dashratha.

Rama and Lakshmana in the garb of warriors along with Vishwamitra began their foot journey. On the way fell tracks, short routes and forest life.

They went on walking long silently. Vishwamitra was walking ahead, and Rama and Lakshmana were following him with the same speed.

"Gurudeva!" Lakshmana broke silence.

"Say, Son!"

"How long do we have to walk like this?"

"Are you tired?" paused Vishwamitra and looked at Lakshmana smilingly.

"I knew you'd say so; but even then I didn't change the language of my question?" There was mischief in Lakshmana's voice.

"Lakshmana!" Rama intervened sternly. It was quite clear from his voice that he was cautioning Lakshmana that his behaviour with Vishwamitra was not conducive to honour.

"Don't stop him from saying , Rama! Let him say-Putting a question doesn't mean disrespecting someone." Vishwamitra was still smiling, "Perhaps you want to know how far my ashrama is."

"Not ashrama but the first night stay. Where shall we stay tonight?" Lakshmana laughed, "Now don't say that Lakshmana is worried about living in a palace."

"You too..."Vishwamitra burst into laughter, "No, I'm not saying this. We'll spend the night on the banks of the Sarayu river."

"Then again the same question arises, gurudeva! How long do we have to walk still?"

"Almost a span of three hours...but you could have asked this in a direct way," Vishwamitra said comically.

"Gurudeva! This is the very thing I'd asked, and that too in a direct way. But you interpreted in a different way."

"But why do you want to know about the time?" Rama too couldn't hide his smile.

"Because if we've to walk together for such a long time, why do we then walk silently like unknown persons? Why don't we talk and crack jokes?" Lakshmana stepped forward to walk farther, "I don't regard him an ascetic if he is gloomy or glum. A mendicant is supposed to be like a fully blossomed flower and happy. Even otherwise I'm not saying this for you. Your wild laughter has made it clear to me that you too like me believe in celebrating life."

"I fully agree with you, son!" Vishwamitra's voice was affectionate and serious. He kept quite for a while. Rama and Lakshmana were looking at him. The facial expressions of Vishwamitra were telling them that he hadn't yet completed his sentence. He had got lost in his inner thoughts for some time.

"Life can be looked at from different angles. Therefore, one's perspective alone should never be regarded as the last one." Looking into the void, Vishwamitra was advancing, "You say that you don't regard a gloomy person a mendicant. I once again agree with you. But, son! if you look at an ascetic who is buried in deep meditation, he will look to you glum and sad. But there's a sea difference between 'sadness' and 'insensitiveness'. A dancing joker can't be a true ascetic."

"Those persons who fled their responsibilities out of fear and became mendicants began to be called respectfully as 'indifferent'. For example, a slightless person can be called a divine-sighted person."

"No, there is a qualitative difference." Vishwamitra's voice became sharper, "only those who rose high above common human faults and other worldly cycles of life were called 'indifferent'. But those who are lost in divine thoughts are also 'indifferent'. Those who are highly seated on the summit of Super-consciousness are too 'indifferent'. All these people are indifferent to worldly desires and ambitions of life."

"Amazing!" Lakshmana got stunned to hear this."Gurudeva! I had never thought from this angle."

"This is why I asked you not to bind yourself only to one perspective. If anyone says that in his view the water falling from mountains wrigglingly and happily is the river, and not the one that flows calmly and indolently on the level ground, what will you call that person?"

"That person will be called ignorant Lakshmana." said Lakshmana.

All the three burst into wild laughter.

"Gurudeva!" said Rama," On many occasions, while talking, Lakshmana forgets the other person's rank, dignity and honour, and gives utmost importance only to the discussion. In such a situation many persons take him to be an angry, rude person. But Lakshmana is innocent. It is his natural simplicity that..."

"Rama," Vishwamitra prevented Rama with his gesture. "It is Lakshmana's special quality, and it is the source of our strength. If he continues talking, time won't hang upon us heavily."

Lakshmana looked at Rama proudly and lapsed into a smile.

"If you have more questions to ask, you can," spoke Vishwamitra. "Don't sustain any hesitation in your mind. Speak what is in your heart as it is."

"Gurudeva! I'm very happy that you've guided me to be fearless." Lakshmana's voice was tinged with respect, "otherwise it's always opposite to it. When we ask our elders any question and if they have no answer to it, they call us uncivil and ignorant."

"I'll not do that because you've already acknowledged you're ignorant." As Vishwamitra said this, the whole atmosphere was charged with laughter.

"My question is why you asked only for Shri Rama for the protection of your yajna."

"Your question is quite right. I should have asked for Shri Lakshmana too." Intentionally Vishwamitra veiled this question's gravity.

"The one who wants Shri Rama knows very well that he'll automatically get Shri Lakshmana without being asked for."

"I bow my head before you for your intelligence, Gurudev!"

"It's not without thinking I've selected Rama." All of a sudden, Vishwamitra leapt out of the ambit of jokes and he revealed it in his voice, "In this context I have studied Rama very minutely. Other kings and their sons are plunged in wine and women. They are simply managing to check demons from creating terror within the bounds of their kingdoms. But it's better to say that they are doing so, not for their kingdoms but only for their palaces. If any simple, ordinary person is vexed by an evil person, nobody comes forward runningly to save him from that person's cruelty. The true Kshatriya is the one who helps the weak and fights for the poor and helpless people."

"Yes, this is what all kshatriyas do!" There was simplicity of a child in Lakshmana's voice.

"No!" There was harshness in Vishwamitra's voice, "Not a single Kshatriya is doing so. Only Shri Rama is the Kshatriya who is doing so. I have done a lot of research on Rama. I've been told that Rama looks after his people like a father. He doesn't tolerate injustice and cruelty. He looks upon everyone with one eye. He makes no difference between one man and another. There is no one like him in crushing the evil persons."

"But you should have said these things to our father, Gurudeva!" said Lakshmana cheerfully, "He still thinks us to be infants."

"Dashratha will see that these very small children who are thought to be sucking their mother's breast will take away the lives of demons." Vishwamitra seemed to be lost in a dream, "Rama! I'll give many divine powers to both of you. I'm confident that you'll never misuse these powers."

"It's your blessing, gurudeva!" said Rama meekly. "Kindly bless us that we're able to get success in our desired mission. But there're certain questions concerning demons in our mind."

"There is no need of taking permission or showing any formality; ask, Rama!"

" Don't those whom you're calling demons belong to human species? It's a general opinion about them that they eat men. They are terrible. They've inexhaustible powers."

"I've heard, gurudeva! that they are well skilled in fighting illusory wars." Lakshmana smiled, "This is what our father says."

"Demons belong to human species."

Vishwamitra paid no attention to Lakshmana's comicality and began to unfold his thoughts, "But it will be appropriate to say that there is nobody else but man who is a demon. These people cheat the helpless. They get pleasure out of their pain and distress. That's why they're called demons. Murderers and dacoits belong to this demon class. They create panic among the weak people by torturing them and killing them so that they may begin to tremble by merely hearing about them."

"I've heard gurudeva!" There was curiosity mixed with excitement in Lakshmana's voice, "that the demons eat away rishis and sages. Is it this story believed in by people or is it something else? Kindly unfold this mystery!"

"Lakshmana!" Flames of fire were rising from Vishwamitra's eyes," There's nothing secret about it. It's absolutely true. Demons eat rishis and sages and make a heap of their bones. Murdering anyone means eating him. But some demons have really become cannibals. In order to demonstrate their terror, they really kill men and eat them."

"Rishis and sages are innocent. Why them?"

"Every person who walks upon the path of righteousness is innocent. Every person is an ascetic who creates awareness about truth among people and who lights the lamp of knowledge in every house. Such a person becomes the victim of unjust and cruel persons. Similar is the case of kings who don't tolerate the intelligent people pointing out their wrong policies. "

"Don't kshatriyas punish demons?" said Rama in his powerful voice.

"Most of the kshatriyas are now looking after their own selfish interests. They've got no connection with the poor and the helpless." There was condemnation in Vishwamitra's voice, "Kings are using their royal power for leading a luxurious life. They reside in their palatial houses and leave their subject at the mercy of their corrupt officials. Consequently, in such kingdoms people suffer."

"Gurudeva!" said Rama, "Rama is taking a vow before you that he'll always discharge his duties as a Kshatriya. Now he'll put an end to the panic created by demons."

"Rama!" Vishwamitra stepped forward and took Rama in his arms. Two tears fell from his eyes, "The world is awaiting you. Protect the poor."

× × ×

It was evening time. The Sun was sinking into the Sarayu river as if to take a bath in it.

Its water was golden in colour. After taking their bath, they came to its bank and sat on mats interwoven with leaves and straws. He noticed that Rama and Lakshmana were picking up leaves and straws quite conveniently and meekly. It looked as if they were forest dwellers, and not princes.

"Rama! I want to give you two divine powers- 'Balaa' and 'Atibalaa'. Many demons tried to learn these two from me but couldn't succeed in spite of their efforts by deceitful means."

"Gurudeva! Are these two powers to be used for launching weapons?" asked Lakshmana.

"No, my son! When you practise these two learnings, you'll feel an amazing power in your body. You'll always be free from all diseases. Ordinary natural needs like hunger, thirst and tiredness won't torment you. Nobody will be able to attack you while you're asleep or not so alert. It's all due to these two powers. The doors of inexhaustible knowledge will automatically open before you. These two learnings will serve as armour for you."

Rama and Lakshmana bowed their heads. Vishwamitra touched them. They felt a sort of divine tremor. They felt as if Vishwamitra were moving speedily in their body in the shape of wind like wind-god. They experienced as if they were illumined with knowledge. They were feeling as if their body was full of great strength. It was such a kind of power that they could even uproot mountains. They felt as if they were travelling in space and the entire universe were enveloping them. They were totally unacquainted with this kind of happening. They had studied only scriptures. But they had simply heard that strength and knowledge could be transferred into other bodies by means of divine learnings. And they had accepted them as a part of mere stories.

"Meditation is over, sons!" echoed Vishwamitra's voice.

Both opened their eyes. The half moon was smiling in the sky. The constellation of stars was glittering. Perhaps it was mid-night.

"In one moment it's mid-night!" startled Lakshmana.

"In meditation even a moment can be equal to many years of the outside world. Time sinks in the depth of meditation." Vishwamitra looked at him affectionately, "Now with the same feelings you lapse into sleep. The rest, the next morning."

* * *

4

At dawn Vishwamitra rose up. His eyes fell upon the sleeping Rama and Lakshmana. Both the brothers were fast asleep lying like small children on the straw mats. A feeling of warm affection was rising in Vishwamitra's heart. He began to think to whom he should pay his gratitude for these sleeping innocence, simplicity and celibacy- to guru Vashishtha, their parents and friends or them. He minutely observed Rama and Lakshmana. He couldn't find any fault in them. Lakshmana was a river flowing from mountains and Rama like a gigantic river flowing deeply and slowly! He kept on looking at them fascinatingly. He was divided into two minds, one part was telling him to wake up both of them and ask them to say their prayers after taking bath,etc. The other part was melting. It wanted Vishwamitra to let them sleep some time more as he had strained them with fatigue. But his first mind didn't let him do so. It wanted the princes to have the flames of practice and detachment rising continuously. It wanted that whatever divine learning he had given to them, its practice was a must for success.

"Rama, the best among men!" Vishwamitra's voice was full of affection and love.

Rama opened his eyes softly. He felt as if he was not sleeping but lying peacefully with his closed eyes. Lakshmana also woke up. Both of them greeted Vishwamitra most respectfully. They performed the rest part of their duties according to Vishwamitra's instructions and proceeded on their outward journey.

There was still time for the evening to fall. They had reached the place where there was confluence of the Ganges and the Sarayu rivers. Nature was in the full bloom of her beauty. The whole atmosphere was fragrant with flowers' smell. At a little distance, they saw an ashrama full of beauty and charm.

"Sire! Whose ashrama is this? It's so pious and fascinating."

Vishwamitra saw that Rama's voice was full of devotional curiosity. He said to himself, 'It's amazing that Rama is charged with divine energies. These are the qualities which even rishis and sages don't get after leading an austere life for lives after lives.But they are all present in Rama naturally.'

"Rama! It's necessary to know ashrama's history if you want to know it fully." Vishwamitra said, "History says that ages ago Lord Shiva used to sit in meditation in this very ashrama. One day Cupid, the god of Love, made an attack upon him. Then Lord Shiva breathed out loudly and looked at him with his furious eyes. Its result was that all the parts of his body got burnt. He was without them. From that day onward he began to be called 'Ananga' i.e. without body. And this place began to be called 'Angdesh'

"It means that Cupid, the god of love, didn't forsake his body. That's why this region is called 'Angdesh'and the sages living in this ashrama seem to be free from all evils of lust, etc."said Lakshmana.

"Yes, Lakshmana! These ashrama's dwellers are very pious and simple-at-heart. You might not have ever come into contact with such sages."

"Is our guru Vashishtha greater or smaller than these?"

"For this, we'll have to make guru Vashishtha stand by them and take their measurement," laughed Vishwamitra.

"I didn't mean this, gurudeva!" Lakshmana felt embarrassed, "I don't know why it so happens. I put a question in one direction and it goes into another direction, having a different meaning."

"No comparison among sages! Whenever we make a comparison, we make one person low- graded and the other a high-graded. Each of them has his own beauty. Vashishtha is a flower of his own type and other sages are of their own. Suppose there are two flowers of different species. How can you say which of them is better? Both flowers blossom. Blossoming in itself is a complete quality, son!"

"Then, gurudeva! Are deep thinking, meditation, analysis, etc.wrong to do?" asked Lakshmana.

"No, Lakshmana!" said Vishwamitra. "It's the sign of awareness. But behind analysis there should be a feeling of love and beauty, and not of hatred. One should keep oneself in balance while making a comparative study. Some values of life are meant for enjoyment. Gradually, you'll learn yourself what is to be compared and what is not."

"Gurudeva! Tonight will be the night of celebration on the river's bank. Today we're in the area of confluence of two rivers. Therefore, it's not one stream, but many a stream will produce the sweet music for us."

Lakshmana looked towards the sky, "O God! Could we have a chance to live in Lord Shiva's ashrama and get benefit of coming into contact with divine souls?"

Smilingly, Vishwamitra looked at Lakshmana. His eyes were shining with love. He turned his face towards Rama, "Rama! Tonight we'll stay at this holy ashrama. We'll share the ashrama- dwellers' activities of prayer and meditation."

"Lord Shiva is kind and merciful. He fulfils our wishes in no time," Lakshmana spoke in his lively voice.

× × ×

Rama noticed that every ashrama dweller was extremely happy at their arrival. Their bones were dancing with joy.

He understood how the senior ashrama -dwellers held Vishwamitra in high respect. That highly acknowledged great man was moving with him and his brother in such an ordinary way, thought Rama. It was he who didn't accept the journey arranged by king Dashratha. He preferred foot journey and never showed any sign of vanity for being great. Really what a wonderful Vishwamitra! It seemed as if he had amity with the whole world. Even if he ever showed his harshness to anyone, it was for his welfare, and the welfare of the whole world.

Rama had seen only Ayodhya's ashrama up till now. He knew that whenever he entered the ashrama, its dwellers were also conscious that he was a prince. They had beautiful feelings for Rama and showed them in their activities and talks. They always made him conscious that he was a prince.

'But here it's totally different. They are all happy at my introduction. They are treating me as if I were their guest. It makes no difference to them whether I am a prince or not,' thought Rama.

Rama was enchanted by their simplicity. There was happiness everywhere in the ashrama. All the ashrama-dwellers sat together when night approached. Vishwamitra entertained them with many of his interesting and fascinating stories.

"After seeing your holy ashrama, it looks that there's no panic created by any demon in this heavenly area," spoke Lakshmana.

"It's not true." The chief of the ashrama became serious all of a sudden, "We dive into the joys of devotion; we, therefore, bear their cruelties and injustices thinking it's all sent by God, and then once again we sink in that devotion. Of course, we're on this side of the river, demons come here occasionally. But if they arrive, they leave no stone unturned in creating panic. They drink our blood and eat our flesh heartily."

"Brother!" There was anxiety in Lakshmana's voice. He said to Rama, "Now we're eager to have a glimpse of demons more than that of rishis and sages. Perhaps you didn't hear what your bow wanted to say to you. It is eager to pierce the chests of demons with arrows. It wants you to swallow them as the god of Death does."

"Lakshmana! Ultimately excitement only shoots up one's blood pressure. Have peace. When time comes, we'll encounter demons."

When they heard Rama, they all laughed and Lakshmana felt ashamed of himself.

× × ×

On the Ganges' bank a beautiful boat was arranged for Vishwamitra's journey by the ashrama dwellers.

"Great Rishi!" the Chief of the ashrama made a humble request to Vishwamitra, "You take with you Rama and

Lakshmana and undertake your forward journey by this boat. Why to delay this auspicious mission. They'll be waiting for you at your ashrama."

"I agree with you," Vishwamitra folded his hands.

The boat moved towards its destination. The wind was blowing speedily. The clothes on body were making a sound. It seemed they were sporting with the wind. The sweet jolts of the boat and the holiness all around made Rama peep into himself. He closed his eyes and got lost in his own thoughts. Lakshmana was looking at the pilot of the boat peacefully and happily. He felt that the sailor of the boat was lost in his skill of sailing the boat in the same way as a musician gets lost in the music of his own instruments.

The rhythmic sound of the waves was increasing Rama's happiness when he was in his meditative state. He felt as if the sound was getting terrible by and by. After sometime he heard a great noise of waves. The noise was so terrible that it seemed as if the waves were at war with each other, and streams of water were falling upon each other. Rama opened his eyes in order to come out of this dreamland. As he opened his eyes, it seemed that the terrible noise had sought one more route to get into Rama's eyes.

"Gurudeva! What kind of noise is this? Where is it coming from? It seems as if many streams of water were engaged in war. Why is there so much noise?" There was an element of surprise tinged with curiosity in Rama's voice. "What's the reason, gurudeva?"

"Rama!" Looking at the streams of water, Vishwamitra said, "There's a beautiful pond on the Kailash Mountain. They say that it emerged because of the strong will of Brahma. A river flows from this pond, and it flows close to Ayodhya."

"The Sarayu!" Lakshmana smiled.

"Yes, the Sarayu!" Vishwamitra said, "The water of the Sarayu river is mixing with that of the Ganga river here. This great noise is because of their confluence. Rama, it's a matchless scene. Control yourself and greet it respectfully.

Both Rama and Lakshmana greeted this place respectfully and devotionally. They felt as if these two holy rivers had their confluence in their hearts.

"Lord! We've come to the south bank of the Ganga. I had been told to take leave of you at your destined place."

"The water behind that big rock is still. Take the boat to that place."

The sailor offered his obeisance to Vishwamitra. Praising him and thanking his stars, he took leave of him.

Rama's eyes fell upon the place where they had got down from the boat. There was deep silence at that place. There was no sign of happiness in that silence. There was only fear and terror reigning. It seemed that the whole region belonged to Lord Shiva. There was a terrible forest yawning before him. It seemed that all around the whole place was infected with evil spirits who were ready to make an attack on those who came there.

Removing his eyes from the forest, Rama looked at Vishwamitra. Both Vishwamitra and Lakshmana were looking towards Rama.

"What did you see, Rama!"

"Gurudeva! I've never seen such an impenetrable forest. It looks as if it were the kingdom of terror. The terrible sounds made by violent animals and birds are intensifying horror. It seems that lions, wild pigs, elephants, tigers, etc. live here. Is it a horrible forest full of creepers and trees of various kinds?"

"Rama! As you look at life from the depth of your heart, you'll notice many novel things. There's a great episode behind every amazing scene. It will be better if you know it." Vishwamitra entered the bounds of the forest.

"Then it will be a matter of great pleasure, gurudeva! We'll get your good company, enjoy sacred nature and hear beautiful stories. We feel as if we were on a dream journey."

Vishwamitra peered into the forest's dense darkness. Every place was like a cave. Everywhere there were horrible wild creepers. It looked as if they were lying in wait for someone's arrival. It sounded as if a goblin with belled anklets on her feet was wandering around. Snakes and lizards were moving about like flies and mosquitoes. Rama and Lakshmana followed Vishwamitra who was moving forward. On the way fell many ruins which were indicating that once there had been grand buildings here. But they all fell victims of time and the roots of trees and creepers.

"Gurudeva! It looks from the ruins that..."

"There had been majestic buildings here at one time," Vishwamitra completed Lakshmana's sentence.

"Yes!"said Lakshmana with his mouth wide open, " then what had happened to this city?"

"There used to be two grand and prosperous districts known as 'Malada' and 'Karusha'." Vishwamitra, it seemed, was well-acquainted with this forest. He was advancing ahead quite fearlessly. "The legend says that after killing Vratrasura, Indra suffered from dirt and hunger. He felt vexed by the consciousness that he had killed a brahmana. When gods and ascetics saw this plight of Indra, they bathed him in the water of Ganga. Indra came out of his misery after the bath. All the gods felt very happy. Indra was once again sacred and healthy as before. Feeling happy, Indra blessed this area. He said, 'Since I am now ridden of dirt and hunger, this place will be called "Malanda" and "Karusha"- "Malanda" because I had dirt on my body and "Karusha" because I came out of hunger.' "

"It means this forest was adorned with two prosperous cities before!" Lakshmana spoke out suddenly, "Did any divine wrath swallow it?"

"It had been prosperous and well-off for a long time. Business, music, art, education, hospitals and many other means of recreation were available here. Prosperity was at its height in both the cities." Vishwamitra added, "But there was a she-demon named Tadaka. She came here with a thousand cruel, strong and terrible demons. They created such a terrible panic in both the districts that most of the people fled the place, and those who dared to stay here were killed and eaten away by Tadaka."

"She is the wife of a demon called 'Sunda' and their sons are Maareecha and Subaahu who are as brave as Indra. This evil-minded Tadaka is the cause of devastation of these two districts and also the birth of this forest. She has a stronghold over this forest which has an area of one and a half miles. She remains safe here and conducts all her demoniac activities. Now this area is known as 'Tadaka Van'."

Looking at the forest, Rama asked, "Are these the same Mareecha and Subaahu who're creating disturbances while Yajna is being performed?"

"Yes!" Vishwamitra said,"Rama! I order you to liberate this forest from the clutches of the demons who create panic. We're going to have our encounter with Tadaka soon. Rama! Keep it in mind that this encounter of ours with Tadaka should send her into the jaws of death."

"Gurudeva! Can a woman create such a horrible panic? I am a kshatriya who has taken a vow to give protection to cows, brahmanas and women. Will it be right on my part to kill a woman? Will it not be a sinful deed? Will the entire kshatriya society not earn a bad name?" said Rama.

"No, Rama! It will never be so. I know your sensitivity will create obstacles before you from time to time; but, my son, if you look at religion from outside and try to understand it, you will always miss the chance. You're supposed to know religion from within. Any type of classification depends on its understanding from within, not on the grounds of body or clan. The natural qualities of a woman are: affection, love, service, etc. But she doesn't have any of them. Instead of these, she is an embodiment of cruelty, murder, kidnapping, drinking wine and eating meat. Such a body can't do any welfare work. As long as she remains alive, she'll destroy things. You should, therefore, liberate Tadaka from this evil body. Rama! Evaluate her not by her body but by her soul. Examine her conduct. The same Tadaka with her son once tried to eat up Agastya Sage, but she couldn't stay before the powerful and revolutionary sage. When Agastya saw the evil deeds of her sons, he declared them to be demons. Then her husband, demon Sunda tried to kill Agastya, but was killed by the mighty sage. This incident made Tadaka more violent. She arrived with her son Maareecha to murder Agastya. But she fled when she saw the wrathful Agastya, and she became a cannibal. Rama! You're a prince. Even if you have to kill a woman for the protection of the subject, you shouldn't hesitate. If a king has ever to do cruel, sinful or guilty deeds for the good of his people, he shouldn't step back. The most important thing is the welfare of people and the extension of goodness. Whatever hurdles come in this auspicious way, the king should deal with them cruelly. History is its proof. Manthara, Virochana's daughter, wanted to devastate the whole earth. When Indra came to know this, he killed her. Similarly, the mother of Shukracharya and Bhrigu's wife wanted to render heaven devoid of Indra; when Lord Vishnu knew this, he killed her. So you should bid good- bye to pity and hatred and kill Tadaka."

Holding tightly the middle part of his bow with his hand Rama said," Gurudeva! My father, Maharaja Dashratha, had advised me before all gurus and diplomats to obey you completely. I don't want to disobey you in any way, and by your orders I'll kill Tadaka. This will be a good deed for me."

"Brother! But where is Tadaka?" laughed Lakshmana, "Do you see anyone in this desolate and lonely forest?"

"Lakshmana! Do you think nobody saw us moving about in this forest which is the stronghold of Tadaka? Even if a bird that enters here from outside is told about by the demons of this place. But we are equipped with weapons. Do you think they don't know about our entry?"

"It means someone is watching us continuously!" Lakshmana was astonished, "The demons of this forest have the information of each step of ours. Gurudeva! You mean to say that we're surrounded by demons."

"Yes!"smiled Vishwamitra.

"Then why didn't the demons attack us?"

"Because Tadaka is more interested in enjoying the taste of killing, and this is her privilege. Rama! Pluck the string of your bow."

Rama pulled and plucked the string of his bow. The entire forest region echoed with its explosive sound. It created commotion among birds and animals who shrieked and screamed.

After a moment or so, they heard the trampling sound of many people running from one part of the forest, but it was only Tadaka who appeared before them.

"Vishwamitra!" shrieked she in extreme anger.

"Rama!" said Vishwamitra," This is Tadaka. Study her carefully."

Then Vishwamitra said to Tadaka, "O Evil Woman! These two princes of Raghukula, Rama and Lakshmana, have arrived here. They are the living images of Death. They'll gain victory upon you."

Tadaka's mouth foamed in anger. She beat her breast shriekingly like a forest dweller and growled,"Today I'll eat up the flesh and bones not only of one ascetic but also of princes. I've got sick of drinking water. Today I'll drink their blood." Tadaka laughed wildly. She was quite confident of eating them up definitely.

Putting an arrow on his bow, Rama said, "Lakshmana! Look at the height of her body and the shape of her mouth. How terrific these are! On seeing this, a soft-hearted person will die. I see no quality of a woman in her. Even then I give her one chance to move back after severing her ears and nose."

Before Rama discharged his arrow, he had on himself a rain of dust and stone pieces. It seemed in a way that some illusory powers were behind this scene. But Vishwamitra told them that it was the illusory war by demons, that is, to make an attack by deceitful means. Rama understood that it was all being done by the demons hiding behind Tadaka. Rama and Lakshmana discharged a volley of arrows at the places wherefrom dust and stone pieces were coming. One could hear that many demons had been killed. Tadaka lost all her senses when she saw this attack.Up till now she had seen people trembling with fear; the man before whom she stood would automatically lose his life by her mere sight; if he delayed in doing so even a little, she would assist him to do so at once. But these two princes knew no fear. They felt happy when they saw her. It seemed as if she were an object of entertainment for them.

"Brother! Look, Tadaka is madly running towards us, holding a very big stone in her hand."

Rama stood still at his own place and kept looking at her. Tadaka felt that Rama, on seeing her horrible and furious face, had become like an insensitive root. She thought that before she attacked Rama with this gigantic stone, he would have breathed his last. Tadaka seemed to be coming speedily, trampling everything on the way like an intoxicated female elephant. Lakshmana looked at

Rama. Before he could take any decision to warn Rama after studying his mental state, Rama's body had become active as if charged with electricity. Nobody knew when Rama put his arrows on his bow and when he discharged them. Lakshmana saw Tadaka's both severed hands lying on the ground. Tadaka couldn't understand how it so happened. She didn't know where her hands and that huge stone went. But in a moment she understood that Rama had cut off her hands with great skill. Screaming out of pain and anger, she pounced upon Rama with the intention of chewing him up with her teeth. Lakshmana cut off her nose and ears in anger. When all other demons heard Tadaka's scream, they appeared there as if by some illusory power and surrounded her. It seemed as if Tadaka had disappeared, and Rama and Lakshmana once again had an assault made by demons with stones. Rama realized that stone-throwing demons were invisible but they were shrieking to frighten them. Rama launched sound-piercing arrows and in no time were killed the demons falling on the ground. The invisible Tadaka also appeared now. Despite her so much misery, Tadaka was confident of eating up Rama. With this ill intention, she pounced upon Rama once again. Rama thought it better not to give her any other chance. So he discharged an arrow from his bow and it pierced her breast. Tadaka took this assault as if it were a dream for her. Her eyes seemed to be telling Rama that a man couldn't kill her. So a question arose in her who he was. With this feeling, her body fell with a thud on the ground.

A loud sound erupted. It was made by other demons to save their lives. Again, there was peace after sometime - the peace arising from fearlessness. Vishwamitra embraced Rama, kissed his forehead and said affectionately, "Auspicious Rama, the Destroyer of Evil Powers! Tonight we'll stay in this forest and tomorrow morning we'll leave for ashrama. Now this forest is free from the curse of death and has turned into peaceful region. Rama! It is only one forest. There are numerous forests of this type wherein monkeys, bears, vultures, nagas, ascetics, sages and ordinary people are waiting for a Kshatriya like you, Rama! You are for them the incarnation of God who has emerged to liberate them from fear and establish peace and happiness. But after a span of ten days I'll take you back to Dashratha as per promise of mine. My area will, of course, be free from fear. But what about the panic created by other demons? Then who will permit you to come to forests?"

"You are right, gurudeva!" laughed Lakshmana. "Brother is devoted to both father and mother. Prince, of course; he isn't. He is only a devotee. If either of them checks him from going, there is no question of going to the forest. Even if he wants to go the forest for amusement, nobody will permit him."

"How can you say so, Lakshmana?"

"Since you've given the demons a call for war, you are their target, not gurudeva. You have murdered Tadaka and God knows how many more demons will be killed by you in the holy ashrama. Now only you'll be worshipped by demons. Demons will ceaselessly think of you 'O Rama! When are you coming to the forests? Come soon! We're starved.'" Saying so, Lakshmana passed his hand upon his belly, "And in such a case Maharaja Dashratha will intensify your security within the boundaries of Ayodhaya. When you walk, you'll be surrounded by bodyguards. What a beautiful scene it will be! Gurudeva has put you in trouble."

"Lakshmana!" scolded Rama smilingly.

"Lakshmana is right." Vishwamitra's voice was serious, "Every king or prince is increasing the number of bodyguards. When the king's bodyguards are increasingly more in number, naturally people's protectors will be decreasingly few in number. People's protectors are only in name, and they too join hands with killers, playing their vicious role."

"Where are protectors these days? Somehow or the other, people are saving themselves. The one who has no means of saving himself gets killed. Rama! Don't think that your Ayodhaya is completely safe and sound. There too your officials create panic like demons. When you are accompanied by the state officials and go out to know the welfare of your masses, many of them don't happen to express their griefs and problems out of fear of cruel officials. Rama! If you want to assess the real condition of people, go out in disguise or all alone. Assure the people that only justice is your real duty. The welfare of people is your royal duty. Rama! After you return to Ayodhaya, don't forget these forests. They are the abode of sages. You must return to the forests to liberate them from these evil demons."

In agreement to it, Rama bowed his head before Vishwamitra . Blessing Rama with his hand, he said, "Whatever Lakshmana has said is true. After today demons will look for you. Today you've crushed a very important mountain connected with the demon tribe. Demons never leave a person if he harms them a little. And you have killed Tadaka. They might have planned to search for you and lie in wait for you. But Rama! I've many divine powers which can keep various kinds of arms and weapons safe. Tomorrow morning I'll give them all to you. The demons suffer from the fear that I may not offer these divine weapons to someone. The one who has these divine weapons of mine will have the potential to gain victory over demons and gods. It's due to this fear they never attacked my ashrama direct in my presence. Even if they did in their illusory way, nobody knew when they attacked and when they took to their heels. They think if they torment and frighten me in this way, they'll be able to have a truce with me."

"Gurudeva!" Shaking his neck, Lakshmana said, "Of course, they'll have a truce with the god of death but not with you."

"Gurudeva! I beg your pardon. Kindly don't interpret my question in any other way. It simply indicates my curiosity. In its backdrop I have no doubt about you."

"Rama! You're always extra careful about your bounds. Without any hesitation you may ask any question. Leave aside your hesitation."

"Why don't you adopt my ways, my brother, Rama? Whatever I want to say, I simply express it. I don't keep anything in my mind. Gurudeva! Did I say anything wrong?"

"Lakshmana, you are so good that you can never say anything wrong."

"Then why don't you ask, brother?"

"Gurudeva! When you're yourself so powerful, why did you go to Maharaja Dashratha for help? You could have fought the demons. If I could kill Tadaka, it was only because of the power of your presence. You protected me from all evils. I felt an invisible power within me."

"Rama! I had read Dashratha's mind. The same question was within his mind. But there are many persons who don't happen to ask any question simply because of their hesitation, fear and courtesy. I'm very happy, son, that you are very eager to know things..."

Vishwamitra paused for a while. Then looking towards the sky, he said, "Rama! I'm an ascetic. It's not my duty to fight. I'm a scientist. I have the knowledge of manufacturing arms and weapons. If you tell any scientist to go to the battlefield and destroy his enemy since he has made these weapons, do you think he'll do or can do? This is the duty of an army general, of a soldier or of a warrior. There's a difference between me and the demons. I want the use of weapons for the protection of the weak. But the demons want to use them to kill others and create panic thereby. I was in search of a warrior who had control over his sense organs, whose mind was his obedient servant and not his master."

Vishwamitra touched Rama and said, "My search is accomplished, Rama! I had you a direct encounter with panic so that you could feel its pain, its fear and its outcome. May God bless you, Rama! May God who is now in His seed form within you sprout into a gigantic tree! I bless you so."

* * *

5

After taking a morning bath and saying his prayer, Vishwamitra asked Rama to sit at a beautiful place in front of him.

"The most renowned Prince, Shri Rama!" There was a touch of joy and pride in Vishwamitra's voice, "May God bless you, son! You proved to be as worthy as I had expected. Tadaka's killing has made me very happy. No Kshatriya was daring to challenge this Tadaka and her sons- Maareecha and Subahu, out of fear. Tadaka-forest is a substitute for death-forest. Through various means I'd sent my request to many kings to come forward to protect common forest dwellers, ascetics, sages and many other non-descript people. But none of them acceded to my request. They said that they didn't want, for the sake of worthless people, to have enmity with demoniac powers that spread panic. In their eyes it was like *'Bull, come and hit us.'* When I saw that kshatriyas were selfish and cowards, I thought that after some time this earth would be ruled over by demons. It was because these demons were not destroying all the kingdoms together. They were devastating them one by one. When any king in his neighbourhood was assaulted, the other king would be statue-like. He would rather be happy seeing that his one enemy was being destroyed. But after some time he himself would become their victim."

"I had heard much about you, Rama! I thought if there was any kshatriya on this earth who was an embodiment of truth, courage and pity, he must be the incarnation of God. If in the midst of selfish kings there is a solitary king who is always ready to work for the welfare of his people will naturally be taken to be an incarnation by the subject. I didn't want you to go astray from your path. I had pinned all my hopes upon you, Rama!"

"I am really thankful to guru Vashishtha and bow my head to him. He has given you education in a right way, keeping the welfare of the world in his heart. He has given you a right type of direction and has put you on the path of truth."

"Gurudeva! I don't ever wish to go back to Ayodhaya. I want to move about in these violence-ridden forests and hunt for each and every demon, and free the common people from fear." Each and every word of Rama was clear and his voice was effective. He added," If you hadn't brought me into contact with common people's woes of life, I would have also spent my life in palaces like other kings. Until I put an end to the panic, I'll not indulge in kingly amusements and recreations."

"So be it, Rama!" Vishwamitra seemed to be contented. He said," Rama! The divine weapons which I'm going to give you today are most probably not owned by anyone on this earth. If any simple-hearted gets these powers, he'll play a devastating role under the control of his uncontrolled sense organs. What these demons are! They are the men who got some powers and then in the madness of their power they started inflicting cruelties upon others. They became demons because of their inhuman conduct. Rama! After receiving these powerful divine weapons you'll become invincible even for gods, demons, gandharvas, nagas, etc. "

Vishwamitra closed his eyes and lapsed into silence. In his meditation he pressed the middle part between the eyebrows of Rama with his right thumb.

Rama had a jolt-like feeling. He felt as if he were sitting in the sky and Vishwamitra was before him. Vishwamitra was looking into Rama's eyes intensely. It seemed as if Vishwamitra's voice echoed in the sky, "O Valiant Raghunandana! Take these great and divine 'Dandchakra', 'Dharamchakra', 'Kaalchakra', 'Vishnuchakra' and very terrible 'Eindrachakra'. Take also Indra's thunderbolt, Shiva's best Trishul, Brahma's 'Brahmashir', 'Aikaki' weapons, 'Modaki' and 'Shikhari'- two very beautiful and shining clubs. Lion-like among men, Rama! Take also the weapons- 'Dharampash', 'Kaalpash', 'Varunapash', etc. I'm giving you dry and wet 'Ashani', 'Pinaak', 'Narayanna' weapons too. Receive 'Aagnaya', 'Vaayavyastra', 'Hayashirda', 'Kroncha' weapons with these two powers.

To help you kill demons I offer you meaningful 'Kankaal', 'Moosala', 'Kapaala', 'Kimkinni' arms too. O Mighty! Get from me the great weapon 'Nandana' and good conch. Also get Gandharvas' weapons to bring someone under your control - 'Praswapan', 'Prashamana', 'Saumya', 'Varshanna', 'Ṡhoshanna', 'Santapana', 'Vilapana', Cupid's invincible weapon 'Maadana', Gandharvas' 'Maanavaastra', demons' 'Mohanaastra'. You're also given 'Taamasa', 'Mahabali Saumana', 'Samvarta', 'Durjaya', 'Mansala', 'Satya' and 'Maayaamaya'(illusory) weapons, the Sun-god's weapon- 'Tejaprabha'; SomDeva's 'Shishira' weapon, Vishwakarma's 'Darunna' weapon, Manu's 'Sheetesh' weapon.

Rama! All these weapons are very powerful and magnanimous, and can assume any form according to one's wish. Own them and take a few more arms- 'Satyavaana', 'Satyakirti', 'Dhrashtra', 'Rabhasa', 'Pratihaartar', 'Praangmukha', 'Avaangmukha', 'Lakshya', 'Alakshya', 'Dradhnaabh', 'Sunaabha', 'Dashaaksha', 'Shatavaktra', 'Dashasheersha', 'Shatodara', 'Padmanaabha', 'Mahanaabha', 'Dundanaabha', 'Swanaabha', 'Jyotisha', 'Shakuna', 'Nairaasya', 'Vimala', 'Daityanaashaka', 'Yaugandhara', 'Vinidra', 'Shuchibaahu', 'Mahaabaahu', 'Nishkali', 'Virucha', 'Saarchimaali', 'Dhratimaali', 'Vratimaan', 'Ruchira', 'Pitrya', 'Somanasa', 'Vidhoota', 'Makara', 'Parveera', 'Rati', 'Dhana', 'Dhaanya', 'Kaamroopa', 'Kaamruchi', 'Moha', 'Aavaranna', 'Jrambhaka', 'Sarpanaath', 'Panthaan' and 'Varunna'. All these weapons are the sons of Prajapati Krashaashva and very effective. Take them all." Vishwamitra became silent for a while and it looked as if he had started some divine prayer.

Rama felt directly that all the weapons given to him by Vishwamitra were expressing themselves embodied. Some of them were like fireballs, some like black smoke; some of them were like sunrays and some like moonbeams.

All these embodied divine arms folded their hands before Rama and said in their meek, sweet voice, "O Lion among Men! We're all your slaves. Magnanimous Raghunandana! We're always at your beck and call. Give us order what we should do for you."

"Reside in my heart, all of you. Whenever I need your help, present before me." Rama touched all those divine arms with his hands. As soon as he touched them, all the embodied divine arms went round Rama and began to enter his heart.

When Rama opened his eyes, he saw that Vishwamitra was not there. Lakshmana was sitting by him.

"Gurudeva left this place a long time ago. He had instructed me to see that no problem arose for Rama sitting in meditation."

"Where has Gurudeva gone?"

"He said that he would return before the evening fell. He has perhaps gone into the forest for solitude."

"Lakshmana! My training seems to be complete today. Most probably no other person will ever be born on this earth like Vishwamitra who is the well-wisher of the world. He has given me his divine arms in a special way. If anybody had told me this in words, my intelligence would have mocked at it and condemned it as a mere figment of mind. But intelligence felt undone before this developed process. Only the pure heart felt activated."

"How are you feeling now, brother?" asked Lakshmana out of curiosity.

"I feel I've become mighty like God. But at the same time I feel that I'm an ordinary man. I am both simultaneously-common and uncommon also; imbued with qualities and without qualities also; gigantic and pigmy-sized also, end too. At present my heart is over brimmed with love and pity. I feel as if I'm the creator of the whole world and also I'm responsible for all weals and woes. The whole world is my extension."

Lakshmana was looking at transformed Rama fascinatingly. It looked as if Rama had been proclaiming this from the summit of Supra Energy. He felt as if God were speaking to him through Rama's heart. Rama seemed to be in meditation of divine world. Lakshmana looked at Rama intently. A wonderful brightness and energy was erupting from every pore of Rama's body. Lakshmana bowed his head before Rama.

Immediately after crossing Tadaka forest., Rama was fascinated by the natural sight.

"Why did you stop, Rama?"asked Vishwamitra looking at Rama.

Lakshmana too looked towards Rama who was staring into something void.

"My Gurudeva!" Rama continued to look towards the same direction and said, "Look there, it looks as if the clouds over that mountain were made of trees instead of vapours. And these dense clouds have covered this mountain.

A pack of thousands of deer seem to be present there. Countless birds flying in the sky are warbling in that area. How melodious is the noise coming from that mountain! On seeing the holiness and faultlessness of that atmosphere, we feel that we've left Tadaka forest far behind. Tell me something about this place, gurudeva!"

"When this place is so enchanting that even brother has lost all his senses in its charm, then there must be some beautiful story around it. Tell us that story, gurudeva!"requested Lakshmana cheerily. He added, "Guru Vashishtha is of serious nature. When we received education from him, he gave us knowledge very seriously. Stories- he also told us but like a meditative person lost in deep contemplation- very slowly, seriously and calmly.

But, gurudeva! you tell us stories in an interesting way."

"Lakshmana! Stop making comparisons," said Vishwamitra smilingly.

"And shrewdly also, Lakshmana!" A smile spread on Rama's face. Vishwamitra laughed wildly.

"Lakshmana, if you really want to hear stories from gurudeva, you can say so in a simple, direct way," said Rama with the same play of smile.

"After returning to Ayodhaya, give Lakshmana the job of a story-teller in a school, Rama!"clapped Vishwamitra.

"If best of men, Rama and best of rishis, Vishwamitra besiege a person, what will be that person's condition. I've already seen. I accept my defeat and surrender myself wholly," Lakshmana bowed his head in a dramatic way.

"Rama! This is the holy ashrama."

"Oh!" Lakshmana had his mouth wide open in surprise.

"Is this the place, gurudeva, where you perform all your activities connected with Yajna? Is it the same place where the sinful, cruel brahma-killing and evil- spirited demons create a dance of blood-shed?

"Yes!" spoke Vishwamitra, "Nobody comes to know when they appear in Tadaka forest and when they disappear again in this forest after assault." Pointing to one track, Vishwamitra said, "This path is too short. We shall reach the ashrama very soon."

"Gurudeva! How did you choose this holy and fascinating place?" asked Rama while walking down the slope.

Vishwamitra looked towards Lakshmana and said aloud so that Rama could hear him, "A beautiful story is connected with this place also. Let me tell this."

"I feel gratified, gurudeva!"said Lakshmana gladly, and he acted as if to dance.

"In ancient times Lord Vishnu used to sit in meditation at this place. Here, every sitting of his in meditation proved fruitful. This is the place where he emerged as the incarnation of 'Vaamana'. Since every meditation proves successful at this place, gods have, therefore, called it 'a holy or fruitful ashrama.' I am boundlessly devoted to Lord Vaamana. Despite his being short- sized, he measured everything in one step. This is the reason why I've chosen this place for my own successful meditation." He turned towards Lakshmana, "Now we are going to get into the ashrama. That's why I shortened this long story. I'll remain silent for the next six days. So, don't be sad and desperate."

Rama saw Lakshmana and smiled.

As Vishwamitra stepped into the ashrama, his happiness grew more and more. Rama and Lakshmana were walking side by side. He took Rama and Lakshmana's hands into his hands like a friend and said in an excited, cheerful voice, "Rama! This ashrama is not only mine but it's yours also. Whatever I had, I've already given that to you."

On seeing Vishwamitra coming, the whole ethos of ashrama was filled with joy. The ashrama dwellers and ascetics surrounded Vishwamitra, and began to leap and bound, and dance. Such a kind of natural welcome had never been witnessed by Rama and Lakshmana. If it had been some other ashrama, there would have been an atmosphere of gravity and seriousness at the arrival of the Vice-Chancellor of the ashrama.

But here it was totally different. He was honoured and welcomed according to the norms of the ashrama.

Vishwamitra sat on a mound under a large tree having the company of Rama and Lakshmana, Kaushika sage, Punarvasu and many other main sages.

Rising from his place, Vishwamitra motioned all other ashrama dwellers to remain silent. The place which echoed with many voices changed into a peaceful place in no time.

"My own People!"said he aloud, "These two princes, Rama and Lakshmana are Dashratha's sons. I went to Ayodhaya for Rama but I got with him even Lakshmana who is brave, chivalrous and plunged in brotherly love. The demon-killer Rama has proclaimed to destroy all the demons."

"Guruji! Will these two princes be able to kill those demons who had slain my father?" asked a boy out of innocence.

"Come here, son!" said Vishwamitra with boundless affection in his voice.

A mendicant took the child in his lap and made him sit on the mound. Vishwamitra patted him. He took his hand in his hands and said, "All of you will be extremely happy and contented to know that yesterday the Valiant and Best among men, Shri Rama awarded death sentence to Tadaka and her accomplices for their sins. Now in Tadaka forest her dead body will be a warning to all other remaining demons."

When ashrama dwellers heard about Tadaka's killing from Vishwamitra's mouth in such a natural way, they began to murmur. Vishwamitra assessed the whole situation by their feelings and expressions, and said, "Let all ashrama-dwellers come to know once again that Tadaka has been killed."

"Hail thee, Prince Shri Rama!" came a happy voice from somewhere. It was followed by many other voices echoing.

Rama rose up from his seat and bowed his head before all the present personages. Vishwamitra motioned them all to be quiet. There was silence all around. Rama cast his love-lorn looks upon the ashrama dwellers and said, "In a short time in this ashrama I have noticed that all the ashrama dwellers hailed Vishwamitra by calling him 'guruji', 'revered guru' and 'gurudev' and not by 'brahmarishi', 'revered rishi' or 'revered sage'. They aren't afraid of his being so great. They are full of limitless love and devotion for him. Just now gurudeva has told me that this ashrama is as much mine as his. Then why are you being partial to me?

Don't make me conscious that I'm not one of you by calling me 'Prince Shri Rama' Simply call me Rama. It's not my victory, it's yours, it's gurudeva's. Gurudeva has told me that the demons cause too much blood-shed in your ashrama. Many ascetics and sages have been killed before time by them. Many of them have been rendered handicapped. I feel agony, pain and woe left behind them. I promise you that I'll destroy these demons by your cooperation. I want that only very necessary persons should take part in Yajna. The rest of ascetics should be ready with me for fight."

"But ascetics are not Kshatriyas. Waging war is not their forte," said a young ascetic out of concern.

"You're right, O ascetic! Fighting war doesn't lie within the nature of ascetics and mendicants. Neither householders nor ashrama-dwellers can fight. But, friends, it is nature's order to protect oneself. If any violent animal makes an attack on your family, will you say that fighting doesn't lie in your nature and then you'll set aside? No, you'll immediately become alert and active to face the attack. You'll never know when you got ready to fight the animal, without caring for your life. Self-defense is in everyone's nature. Demons have always taken advantage of this weakness of yours. Its result is that demoniac powers have strengthened themselves and godly powers have scattered. Unless and until saints and sages get organized, the evil-minded bodies will exhibit their daring nature."

Rama looked at Vishwamitra and said, "Gurudeva! Today itself you may initiate yourself into Yajna confidently. This holy ashrama will be worthy of its name. Your forecast about demons will prove to be true."

Rama greeted Vishwamitra, other sages and ashrama dwellers, and took his seat.

Vishwamitra took a general view of all ashrama-dwellers. It seemed as if he was casting his looks upon each person for a moment or so. He broke his silence and said, "Whatever Rama has said is to be put into practice. Violence is not our creed, but self-defence is our pious duty. Tomorrow morning I'll initiate myself into Yajna. I'll remain silent for six days. Kaushik sage is with you for further instructions and Rama is present to face demons. Your welfare lies in carrying out whatever they say."

Vishwamitra looked at an ascetic. He blew his conch. It meant that the meeting was over and all should go back to their respective places.

* * *

6

Tadaka's personal demon party's chief, Yamapasha along with his associates was running frantically. As soon as the night fell, he told other demons to fetch Tadaka's corpse. He was running with his bodyguards to break the news of Tadaka's unexpected killing to her son Maareecha and the cousin Subaahu. He was terrified as well as happy. He was frightened because he had seen any man kill demons for the first time. He himself was badly injured because of that man's arrows. Blood was flowing from his body and he could still hear in his heart the piercing cry of Taadaka and visualise how she had felt tormented before she died. He was happy too because he thought that as a reward he would be made the chief of a large battalion of demons when Maareecha and Subaahu came to know that he had not been hesitant in laying down his life for the protection of Taadaka. He was already feeling the joy at his prospective promotion. He was confident of becoming the chief of Taadaka-forest.

This forest is so much ill-famed for panic that by mere citing its name they would pick up anything from a king or an ashrama or a village. Not only this, they kill one or two innocent persons also before departing from there in order to prove how terrific they are.

He was imagining that on the day of his promotion there would be a grand celebration. Beautiful Arya girls would be kidnapped from different states. He would enjoy them and the demons under him would be free to have sexual intercourse with ashrama's girls, nagas, rikshas, monkey girls, etc. Tank's water would be mixed with liquor. All demons would play in it and drink it. While he was lost in his dreams, he reached the impenetrable place where Maareecha and Subaahu had their camps.

All were acquainted with Yamapasha. But when all the chief demon guards saw him so much wounded and frightened, they felt undone. He was running towards the theatre, crying and shrieking.

When the guards of the theatre saw Yamapasha in this plight, they stood aside like other demons.

Maareecha and Subahu immersed in wine and plunged in kidnapped women, were enjoying their life. There were other demons also who were intoxicated with epicurean life. Singing and dancing were at their full bloom. Maid-servants were serving them wine from pitchers and pots.

"O King of Demons! Everything is destroyed. There is deluge everywhere," shrieked Yamapasha with his full might followed by other demons who had accompanied him, "Protect us, Demon king!"

"It's all destroyed," Yamapasha beat his chest.

For a little while the demoniac celebration stopped. All the eyes were fixed upon Yamapasha. He was smeared with blood. His clothes were torn here and there. The ornaments lying on his body were in a disorderly state.

Subaahu looked at him with his drunken eyes and smiled. His smile lapsed into laughter, and laughter turned into its wildness. All the demons gazed at Subaahu to know its reason. Subaahu's laughter was so wild that he began to roll and shouted, "Look at Yamapasha! The Chief of Taadaka's demon army got injured by a wild dog and now he has come over here to take shelter."

As Subaahu said so, all the demons got a chance to mock at Yamapasha. With the gestures of their fingers mockingly, they laughed.

"I've not been bitten by any wild dog," screamed Yamapasha.

"Then does it mean that a monkey has torn your clothes?"echoed a voice. It was followed by a terrible noise of wild laughter again.

"Not a monkey." Yamapasha was feeling ashamed of himself at his misery. He felt strongly inclined to eat up the laughing assembly of people. He felt insulted thinking that those demons who stood before him with their bowed head were now making fun of him.

"Then it may be a bear or a wolf!"

"No... No..."

"Not even a bear?"

"Not even a wolf?"

"Then who else?"

"Why, it may be some man- killing lion."

"Stop nonsense, all of you!" shouted Maareecha. "It seems to me that a man-killing deer has wounded him."

As soon as Maareecha said so, all the demons burst into uncontrollable laughter. Someone lifted his maid and began to dance. Many demons, mad with laughter, made discourteous motions of their fingers.

Now Yamapasha stood still. Laughing at his own insult, he noticed all the demons. He said to himself, 'Laugh at your heart's content. When I tell you about Taadaka's murder, you'll all urinate here in fear.'

When all stopped laughing, Subaahu came to him to ask, "Tell us what Maareecha says that a man-killing deer has wounded you is true. If it isn't true, does it mean that a man-killing female deer has injured you?"

At Subaahu's mischief, laughter at Yamapasha had its repeated occurrence.

"No, it wasn't a female deer. There were two man-killing male deer," came Yamapasha closer to Subaahu and screamed in anger.

"O.K.!" Subaahu's eyes widened out of surprise. "Then why have you come to me after getting injured from those deer? You should have gone to my mother, Taadaka to take shelter in her hem."

This time's outburst of laughter put to shame the whole chain of previous laughter.

"I did try to seek your mother's hem to take shelter in, but before I was wounded those two deer and their hunter ate up Taadaka." Yamapasha was trembling in anger.

Suddenly the whole atmosphere became grave. Subaahu came closer to him, wrinkled up his forehead and said, "What did you say? Are you so dead drunk that...?"

"Narcotic drink, I haven't taken but you and this entire demon society that doesn't happen to see the wave of devastation advancing towards them. I have been crying for a long time." Yamapasha was getting out of control, "But you've no respite from your luxurious life. When that Vishwamitra devours us, only then you'll repent. That Vishwamitra with the help of his two ordinary men chopped off both the hands, nose and ears of Taadaka, your mother and our ladyship and then pierced her breast with a serpent-like terrible arrow."

Subaahu shrieked. He pulled a sword suspending from a demon's back and the next moment he beheaded Yamapasha. His cut-off head was lying on the ground and witnessing everything. His mind was active. It calculated and said, 'Blood is coming out in jets from the upper part of your body and Subaahu has rewarded you.'

Yamapasha's lips murmured, "It's true we're cruel." It was his last shriek, "There will be complete havoc."

Subaahu looked at the demons who had accompanied Yamapasha. He spoke to other demons, "Look, these fellow demons of Yamapasha are now trembling with fear here. If Yamapasha was telling the lie in his intoxication, this was the just punishment for him. And if it is true, then...then... is true... nonsense!" He gave a jolt to his mind and said, "No, it can't be true. We don't count men in any category. Man is regarded as feeble, base and timid in our culture and society. Do you think that man will be able to kill Taadaka? No!"

"What's the truth?" Maareecha came closer and looked at the remaining demons, "Cast aside your fear. The one who was to be punished has been punished. Speak the truth."

"Yamapasha was telling the truth. Vishwamitra brought with him two men, well-equipped with arms and weapons. And they both destroyed everything in no time."

"Where were your weapons?" Maareecha peeped into their eyes.

"If it's true, why did you come here alive? Why didn't you fight the enemy?" Subaahu screamed and rose up.

"It looked from the way those two Kshatriyas launched their arrows from the bows that death was sure and shot," rose up a demon with a trembling voice.

"Even now death is certain," Subaahu raised his sword.

"Stop!" Maareecha said in an authoritative voice.

Subaahu understood that his order was stern.

"Speak further."

"As our ladyship Taadaka entered Taadaka forest, our spies had informed her about the presence of Vishwamitra and the two well-armed men, but she didn't take it seriously. She said that men were small insects and worms for her. If they had weapons in their hands, it exposed only their fear."

"O Demon King!" another demon mustered up his courage to speak, "Vishwamitra was wishing these two princes of Raghu dynasty well and victory. The chief warrior was being called by the name of Rama."

"Princes!" Maareecha was taken aback and said, "How is it that these princes who lead a life of pleasures and luxuries have so much divine power?"

"Maareecha! This is only a dream." Subaahu laughed, "or these soldiers have paid a rich price for their lives and come to mock at us!"

Just then there was some stir caused by someone's arrival. Many demons were coming with a corpse. They placed it on the ground. There was complete silence in the assembly. Maareecha and Subaahu were stunned. It was the dead body of their mother, the mistress of Taadaka forest. She was a great leader, Taadaka, who could take away the lives of her enemies by her mere presence. It appeared from her ruined body that a demon was the most powerless creature.

"Oh!" Maareecha felt as if he wasn't within himself. "The severed neck of Yamapasha has truly said - Havoc. The killing of Taadaka means that a great secret mission to destroy all demons has taken a final shape and they have been totally ignorant of it. It means our spies are always in intoxication."

"Maareecha, there will be total annihilation, but not ours. It will be of Vishwamitra and his entire ashrama, of the remaining ascetics and sages. All the soldiers should get ready for a war mission. Order all the demons to convert the ashrama into mortuary."

"Subaahu! You are always blind with anger." Maareecha scolded him, "Mother also did the same and the result is in front of us. What do you think that Vishwamitra is standing with garlands and waiting for us? Somehow or the other he is quite confident that he will not only make a counter attack on us but also destroy us. First of all, we must perform final rites according to demons' system in the honour of our mother who is the pride and glory of our demon culture. Then send the spies to the ashrama to assess the whole situation there. After that, we'll make a strategy of attack."

Subaahu was mad with anger. He threw his sword with full might on the ground and broke it. He screamed and declared to kill Vishwamitra.

"Subaahu!" Staring into the void, Maareecha said in his stern voice, "Try to understand two reasons why the demons couldn't harm Agastaya and Vishwamitra. The first reason is that they are in possession of divine arms which return to the owner after hitting the target. As a result, we are not benefitted by it. The demons believe that by swindle and fraud, they will, if not today then tomorrow, be able to steal these divine weapons."

"But it may also happen that if anyone uses these divine arms, our side will suffer a great tragedy as you can see just now before us. Vishwamitra has got this work done after transferring all his power to an ordinary prince. But who is such a prince whom Vishwamitra trusts so much that he won't feel tempted to make use of this great power? We'll make all our efforts to capture those two princes and force them either to become demons or be ready for death sentence."

"Vishwamitra!" screamed Subaahu in fear and anger, and then fell upon Taadaka's dead body.

*   *   *

7

Today was Yajna's last and sixth day. In the last six days Rama got the information about all the activities of demons from Kaushik sage and adjusted the security system accordingly. Rama himself was stationed in the main and sensitive area and the security of the rest part of the ashrama was being looked after by Lakshmana accompanied by the group of young ascetics.

"Today the demons will definitely attack the ashrama," said Kaushik sage. He added, "God knows who is their spy in our ashrama that gives them information about our activities. When I go round the ashrama for inspection, I feel it's all my doubt. Here there is not a single benefactor of demons. And when I note the timings of their assault, I feel that somebody is telling them when to launch an attack on us."

"In the past six days we didn't have any smell of any demon. But when a cowboy went into Taadaka forest to know their secrecy, he told us that a large army of demons had gathered there like locusts and that they are moving towards us quite cautiously. He said that they knew that today's Yajna was at its height and so there was every possibility of their attack on the ashrama today itself."

Just then Lakshmana was seen coming towards Rama.

"Speak out!"asked Rama.

"It is certain that demons will attack us today. Why should we then throw the young ascetics into the jaws of death unnecessarily? If they showed even a little bit of carelessness, they would all be killed. You and I alone can convert this war into our victory," said Lakshmana.

"It's not the question of gaining victory in the war, Sumitranandan!"said Rama. "It's the question of instilling courage in men, particularly the sufferers. Rama will also help those who are excited to help themselves. No doubt, today I'll fight for them, but who will then fight for them tomorrow? Every time they should be dependent upon others for their safety- I don't want this. When we weren't here, the demons killed many in this ashrama. If today a few more sacrifices are made, then why this fear? It's a sin to be fear-ridden and get oneself killed while living at the mercy of others. Virtue lies in laying down their lives while fighting in the war. The mothers whose sons sacrifice their lives in the war feel proud of themselves, and the mothers whose sons lose their lives in an ordinary way are grief-stricken. I want to infuse self- confidence in them that they have themselves won the war. Rama's presence was only a trifle."

"May God bless you, Rama!" Kaushik sage said, "You are not only a man of action but also you are empowered by the might of knowledge."

The Yajna was at its climax. All the ascetics and sages sitting there were happy. It never happened that any yajna had continued to be performed for six days without any hindrance. Before the sages began their research of any kind, the demons would make their presence feel and destroy the whole thing. They felt that after Taadaka's killing all the demons had fled towards south.

Just then there was a great commotion outside the ashrama. The ashrama-dwellers were crying and running pell-mell. The heart of the ascetics sitting within the campus of yajna site was palpitating out of fear. But Vishwamitra had given clear instructions to all that nobody would run away, leaving the yajna for fear of demons. Howsoever demons came closer to them, they should remain engaged in performing yajna like a bumble bee sucking the essence of flowers whole- heartedly.

"Look, Rama! Just as the sky is overcast with clouds in the rainy season, in the same way the demon army is advancing from all the four directions to devour the ashrama. Look there, Maareecha and Subaahu, the mightiest demons, are progressing towards the yajna site." Kaushik sage's voice was calm and there was no trace of uneasiness on his face. It seemed as if he had taken a decisive decision- the ashrama would be safe and sound forever after this or there would be no vestige of it at all.

In the direction of Yajna site Maareecha saw Kaushik sage standing with two armed young men pointing to them."Subaahu! These are two kshatriya princes - Rama and Lakshmana. They are the sons of Dashratha, the king of Ayodhaya. The spies have told us that they are youngsters. These are only children. But their physical stature tells us that they are very strong." Maareecha expressed his assessment.

"Man doesn't have strength. See how I kill them and make their offerings at Vishwamitra's Yajna-fire. Today we'll see the might of Vishwamitra also. We've waited long."

Rama sent Lakshmana to protect the rear part of the ashrama. Lakshmana started shooting a volley of arrows, as if electrified, at the demons who were going to the rear part of the ashrama. Even the terrified ascetics were filled with excitement when they saw many demons being killed together. They too started fighting them fearlessly. Lakshmana noticed that one group of demons was throwing the blood and cut-off parts of animals' bodies. He understood that they did so in order to intimidate the soft-hearted forest dwellers and lessen their mental strength. After killing the innocent people they dipped themselves in their blood.

The demons were equipped with swords, daggers, heavy clubs, knives, saws, etc. They perhaps didn't know the value of bow-arrows or they never felt their need. Hence they fell down like chopped trees when they advanced shoutingly. The demons began to run pell-mell. It looked as if Lakshmana were enjoying the fight. His eye-sight was sharp and with his wonderful physical quickness he was busy shooting arrows.

Rama killed all the demons who were accompanied by Maareecha and Subaahu with his volley of arrows. Such a kind of skill Maareecha and Subaahu had probably heard of only in stories. They stared at Rama. It looked as if their eyes were trying to discover the invisible power in an ordinary prince called Rama. But they didn't like the idea of running away from there. They simply looked at each other.

"We should have used the services of our bowmen," said Maareecha. "I had never imagined such a kind of scene."

"If we had sent Ravanna, the King of Lanka, the message that he should send his demon bowmen to kill two ordinary men, he would have got us killed. In his eyes, the one who is afraid of man can't be a demon. And the one who is not a demon has no right to be alive." Subaahu waved his sword in the air and ran towards Rama shriekingly. Maareecha too did the same.

Rama took out a deadly man-made arrow called 'Sheeteshu' from his quiver and ordered it to make an attack on the target with full might and wound it without destroying it. He pulled the string of his bow, turned it towards Subaahu and then suddenly towards Maareecha and released it. The terrible assault made by the arrow pushed Maareecha with so much force that he fell down in the same manner as a person falls down rollingly from a speedy chariot. One could see fear in the dilated eyes of Subaahu. He paused to see the plight of Maareecha who was crying in agony. He raised himself, and like a mad man swung round so speedily as if he were a mad dog who had held its tail in between its teeth and swung round in a circle.

By that time another party of demons arrived all of a sudden.

"Take away the wounded Maareecha immediately to the demons' camp situated on the sea coast and get him cured immediately by the skilled physicians. In no time will I destroy this ashrama."

On receiving orders, that demons'party took away Maareecha in the twinkling of an eye. And then suddenly another demon group appeared. Subaahu felt encouraged.

"O you cruel, bad charactered, sinful and blood thirsty demons! You have no right to live on this planet. The vase of your sins is full up to the brim." Rama made all the demons aware of the results of their sinful deeds. He summoned the wind-branded arrow and released it at the demons. When

Subaahu saw his men being killed, he lost his courage and so he fell upon Rama with his full might.

It appeared as if Rama was already prepared for this attack. He put the fire- branded arrow on his bow, closed his eyes in contemplation and released it at Subaahu. The arrow hit Subaahu's chest. There was a terrible explosion and Subaahu's chest broke into pieces like a burst water melon. Demons took to their heels. When the ashrama dwellers saw them running away like this, they were filled with courage. They chased them and whichever demon fell into their clutch, he was killed. The ashrama dwellers' joy echoed limitlessly. They surrounded Rama and Lakshmana to express their gratitude. After the yajna was over, Vishwamitra came there. He was accompanied by his associate ascetics and sages. He stepped forward and clung Rama and Lakshmana to his heart. In his proud voice and with tears in his eyes, he said, "Rama! I'm grateful to you. You are well-renowned and full of strength. You've proved the worth of this ashrama by killing demons. You have carried out guru's orders fully. The entire humanity is thankful to you." He patted Lakshmana and embraced him. He said affectionately, "Lakshmana! Your arrows are speedier than your words."

The entire campus burst into laughter.

"It's your blessings, gurudeva!" Lakshmana was extremely happy.

"Gurudeva!" spoke Rama in his most modest voice, "Both of us are at your service. If there is any further order for us, please say."

"I am very happy with you, Rama! There is one more thing in my mind but I'll talk about it next morning after the performance of yajna. Till then you enjoy yourself in the company of forest dwellers. I make an arrangement of the cremation of demons' corpses."

× × ×

Vishwamitra who was present in the midst of rishis was engrossed in discussion. Rama and Lakshmana greeted them all and addressed Vishwamitra, "Gurudeva! Speak out your heart."

"O Son of Raghu dynasty!' Vishwamitra said, "I have now decided to leave this ashrama and go to Himalayas. But ashrama dwellers are worried and desperate because of this decision of mine. I know my duty is over. Now I want to break the bonds of love. The same thing I was telling them that they should take the charge of the ashrama and be capable of protecting it. Neither I nor Rama has forsaken them. Rama will always remain sensitive to their security. I have assured this thing also to them. But God knows why they feel insecure and unsafe if I go to the Himalayas and Rama returns to Ayodhaya. They fear that when Rama on his return to Ayodhaya gets busy in his kingly duties, he'll forget them."

"Gurudeva, everything is clear to me." Rama said in his appealing voice, "Why do you want us to wander through forests and kill demons? Don't the ashrama dwellers understand this simple thing?" Rama looked at ashrama dwellers and said aloud, "Faultless and chaste ashrama dwellers! I am grateful and indebted to gurudeva who brought me in contact with common people and made me know the cruelties inflicted upon them in a direct way. Gurudeva has introduced me to truth and has told me what the real duties of a king are. He has guided me that a king's real happiness lies in the happiness of his people. He has brought me in contact with the pain which I could never have experienced in the kingdom for being surrounded by my bodyguards. Friends! The truth is that I had been feeling insatiated for a long time. I had begun to put questions to guru Vashishtha out of so much curiosity that everyone grew suspicious thinking that I was perhaps going to leave the house to become a mendicant. I peeped into myself at the blessed feet of gurudeva Vishwamitra. I'm telling the truth that I've seen my real image. I find that I'm not different from you in any way. It is my promise that I will never ignore the poor and the helpless."

"The Well-wisher of the poor! Victory to Shri Rama!" arose the echoed voice of happiness in the ashrama as if it were the deluge of eulogy.

Vishwamitra rose up and clung Rama to his chest. In this posture they remained for a long time. Kaushik sage gestured with his hand to all to be quiet.

"Rama!" Vishwamitra placed his hands on both the shoulders of Rama. Gazing into his eyes, he said, "My ardent desire is to take you to Mithila. King Janaka has an ancient Shiva-bow as a legacy. It's on top of all the divine arms that I have given to you. Lord Shiva has activated it many times in the war. It has been lying unused in the museum like a wonderful object for ages together. I want you to bless yourself with the sight of this scientific object of wonder. Then I'll undertake my journey to Himalayas after handing you over to Dashratha.

"I am present, gurudeva!"

"Not 'I' but 'we'!" Lakshmana gave a comfortable twist to the whole situation feelingly.

"Rama! Our revered Vishwamitra was telling us that you never disregarded his desire. Doesn't it mean that there is no refusal in your heart and mind?"

Rama speechlessly looked towards Kaushik sage as if he were thinking whether he should give an answer to that question. It was because no answer arose within him.

"Shall I give you its answer, great sage?" asked Lakshmana. After getting permission he said, "I have noticed two elements in brother Rama- which are like the two wheels of a chariot running at the same speed. These elements are 'Devotion' and 'Courage'. What a wonderful quality or skill he has, to leap into the unknown!"

"Very beautiful answer you gave, Lakshmana!" Vishwamitra patted him on his back affectionately. He addressed Kaushik sage, "Kaushik ji! Arrange for our journey to Mithila."

× × ×

8

On reaching Mithila, the King Janak's chief priest Muni Shataananda, came to meet Vishwamitra. He greeted them all and with his tearful eyes he looked at Rama. There were tears of gratitude and love in his eyes. He said in his hoarse voice, "Rama, you are great. You freed my mother Ahalya from her accursed and pathetic life she had been leading for ages together. God knows what people said about her. Some said that Ahalya was attracted to Indra and had accepted his call for lustful life. Some said that intoxicated with his power and might Indra had inflicted cruelties upon my mother. I don't know where truth lies. I was then only an ignorant child. I knew only this much that even my father, Rishi' Gautama had held my mother guilty. He had abandoned her out of fear of the society and the other members of the society too had forsaken her, taking her to be sinful. And she continued to lead a forsaken and humiliated life. She was declared to be untouchable by the society. She was turned out of the caste. I heard that people had started saying that Ahalya lost her consciousness and turned into a stone in her solitude, Rama!"

It appeared that Shataananda would burst into tears like small children. He said, "Rama! I'm Shataananda who was born from Ahalya's womb and her blood and breath brought me up. I am a part of her soul. I am unfortunate, timid Shataananda who took no step in getting her rights back. I too kept quiet for fear of the society. But Rama! You're the living image of fire. You aren't scared of society's untruth or people's ill words. You are the embodiment of truth, the incarnation of righteousness, Rama!"

"No, great sage! I am also an ordinary person like you. I know only this much that I can't brook falsehood and injustice."

"Rama! When I came to know that you entered the terribly peaceful forest which was like the cremation ground and touched the feet of my mother and my father accepted her, I had wept bitterly. Rama! You've freed me from my burden." Shataananda grew emotional and said, "Now everywhere there is a talk today and the belief that the woman who has been touched by Prince Rama, the best of men and the pride of Raghu dynasty can't be sinful. You are indeed the one who can make even the sinful chaste and pure, Rama!"

Rama stepped forward and embraced sage Shataananda. Muni's emotional tears flowed without any obstacle.

Vishwamitra and Lakshmana too saw this emotional moment with tears in their eyes.

"Rama!" Vishwamitra called, "Come here! Shataananda, you also come here."

Rama and Shataananda sat beside Vishwamitra.

"Do you know, Shataananda, that intentionally I took Rama to the Ashrama of the ousted mother of yours. Before this, I had told him the full story about the injustice done to your mother. I wanted to see whether Rama who had up till now obeyed me fully could take his own decision in favour of truth that had been set aside by the human society out of fear. I found Rama to be the best of men who lived within his honorable limits. In the entire world of today's Kshatriya society Rama shines brightly like the Sun. They find Rama an ideal kshatriya king who doesn't feel haughty in killing demons."

"Rama! Nobody else will be as great a king as you are. This is Shataananda's blessing springing from his soul. The world will never witness such a virtuous, courteous person. You are the well-wisher of the poor, the purger of the sinful persons and simple, Rama!" Shataananda wiped his eyes with his palms.

"Great Sage!" Lakshmana laughed, "What a beautiful blessing of yours! Why, you hurled a curse upon the world." Peals of laughter changed the whole ethos of the campus which was surcharged with emotions.

"Great Rishi! Now I would like to take leave of you. After a while, I'll come again before you in the company of King Janaka."

Vishwamitra raised his left hand by way of blessing as a token of permission.

Immediately after the departure of Shataananda, Vishwamitra was lost into something unknown.

Rama and Lakshmana were looking at him; but he didn't know about it. After a short while, Lakshmana wanted to pull him out of his dream world. He said aloud, "Gurudeva! Gurudeva!'

This disturbed Vishwamitra's contemplation.

"What are you thinking of, Gurudeva?"asked Lakshmana.

"You had asked me a question, Lakshmana!"

"Gurudeva! But I had asked you many questions," smiled Lakshmana. "Not simply many. There will be no exaggeration if I say that I had asked you a volley of questions one after the other."

This made Vishwamitra laugh. But as it came, it vanished. He again became grave and said, "There was one more important reason why I chose Rama. At that time I didn't express it. But since I'm now going on my last journey, I think it better to speak out what lies buried in my heart."

Rama and Lakshmana were looking at Vishwamitra innocently. Vishwamitra gazed at them and said, "Your guru Vashishtha is really great. Perhaps you don't know that I tried my best to torment and ruin him when I was intoxicated with my powers. But he rendered them fruitless by means of his brilliance of soul. Since I had gained a lot of powers, I had become terribly haughty. In other words, I may say that I degraded myself to the lower status of a demon. Inspite of this, Vashishtha ji never harmed me by means of his divine powers. He gave me many opportunities to come back to the same high status. After introspection I realized how low I had fallen..."

He paused for a while, "I found the demons, after receiving powers, were inflicting tortures upon people in all directions. There was not a single valiant kshatriya who could brave them. One should be brave as well as self-restraint. It was because I had only one fear, and it was that after destroying demons, the Kshatriya whom I trained might not become a demon. I heard about Rama's popularity and when I turned my head to this side I found Rama to be the beloved pupil of guru Vashishtha. Just then like a flash of lightning a thought came into my mind that Rama's journey was approaching nearer. So at the very first sight I understood Rama from within completely. I thought that when a resolute kshatriya and rishi like me couldn't control himself after achieving powers, it meant that it was beyond the control of a man to have a restraint over his powers. It is only God who can keep such huge powers. Decidedly God has descended into Rama."

He looked at Rama and said, "Rama! I see within you God-like seeds sprouting. Always have a feeling of cooperation while these sprouted seeds bloom into flowers. Continue to make attempts to let this sapling grow into a gigantic tree. From the point where you stand the journey of life divides itself into two currents. One is upstream which leads to godliness and the other is downstream which leads to animality and demonship. It is not exclusively with you; it is connected with every person. But the man doesn't happen to see this because of illusion and vanity overpowering him."

He took in a deep breath and lay down in a state of rest, taking the support of pillows. He closed his eyes. Turning his face towards the ceiling, he said in a voice as if it were coming from his contemplation, "Rama! I clearly see your name will be taken as God's in the years to come."

× × ×

Maharaja Janaka came with his ministers and priests to greet Vishwamitra. Lakshmana cast his profound looks upon Janaka. He saw that Janaka's body was vivacious and animated. His face mirrored his heart's joy. His white hair and beard were resplendent like moonlight. His eyes were transparent. He was imbued with divine glory of rishis and munis. It seemed as if something unknown had enshrined itself in him, quite separated from his body. Lakshmana felt as if gulled by his divine qualities.

"Brother!" He whispered into Rama's ears, "we have seen many kings but here it appears that a mendicant is enthroned as a king. We can feel the inner energy rising from within him. You'll agree with me that such a kind of energy has been seen in guru Vashishtha and gurudeva Vishwamitra. Same kind of fragrance, brother! Our father is also a king and Janaka too! But there's a sea difference in both of them."

"Shall I tell gurudeva about your comparative study?" Rama looked at Lakshmana obliquely to tease him smilingly.

"Brother, it doesn't behove a kshatriya to summon a divine weapon and use it for an ordinary thing," Lakshmana threw a dice against Rama.

Rama smiled in joy.

"Son Rama!" Janaka stepped forward and took Rama's face in his hands. He kissed him on his forehead and took Rama in his arms.

Rama was full of hesitation. He thought he should have first greeted Maharaja Janaka but Lakshmana engaged him in his talks. He was still thinking that Janaka was full of praise for Vishwamitra and it could take some more time. But he didn't know how time passed while talking to Lakshmana.

As Janaka loosened his gentle grip, Rama bent to touch his feet. But Janaka didn't allow him to do so. He again embraced Rama and said, "No, Rama! Your place is not in my feet but in my heart. You should enshrine yourself in my heart."

"Son Lakshmana!" He turned towards Lakshmana.

Lakshmana touched his feet and Janaka had no problem in it. After this, he took Lakshmana in his arms as he had done with Rama.

"Rama!" As Janaka sat on his seat, he said, "Shataananda ji has already told us about your chivalry, liveliness, chastity and simplicity. We look upon you as a hero among the Kshatriyas and the common masses."

"This is all gurudeva's greatness. We thank our stars that we got an opportunity to serve him. Gurudeva has instructed us to discharge our duties within our limits. We are walking upon the guided path with the blessings and love of the wise people like you."

"Aha! Wonderful!" Janaka was extremely happy, "I have already expressed my gratitude to gurudeva who brought you here. Even otherwise, wherever gurudeva has gone, there has been an ascendency of someone's stars. God knows how Mithila will be blessed!"

I have seen the ascendency of demons' stars the most," said Lakshmana mockingly. "They feel undone by the mere mention of gurudeva."

The whole place echoed with everyone's laughter.

"Janaka!" Vishwamitra's voice became somewhat serious.

"Command me, gurudeva!" Janaka folded his hands.

"I've initiated Rama to different kinds of divine weapons. I want Rama to have a look of Shiva-bow kept here from ancient times. Its sight will be an auspicious sign. Please arrange for Shiva-bow as quickly as possible and we want you to tell us a beautiful story connected with this bow." He smilingly looked at Lakshmana.

Rama also looked at Lakshmana in the same style.

Lakshmana felt embarrassed.

Janaka instructed the officials concerned to bring the Shiva-bow at once to its destined place. Looking at Rama, he said, "This bow is kept at a very safe place. It's beyond the reach of common people. Only very special and brave Kshatriyas have been able to see it. There are certain reasons for keeping it safe. This bow had been given to my ancestor, Devraja as a legacy by gods in ancient times and there is no sense in making it public to anyone. This bow is indeed, a sophisticated divine weapon. But only Lord Shiva knows how to launch it. We can assess its amazing powers by the fact that nobody has up till now been able to move it even. Being familiar with its divinity, I proclaimed that my brought-up daughter would be given in marriage only to the one who was really a chivalrous person. My condition was that whosoever was able to pull its string, he would be allowed to marry Sita. Who doesn't want to establish relations with such a mighty kingdom as Mithila is?

Therefore, an army of kshatriya princes came to fulfill my condition. But all the princes, intoxicated with vanity and arrogance, proved to be utterly unsuccessful. So they had to return to their kingdom empty- handed. These kings felt insulted, thinking that I had taken this decision to insult kshatriya society. They were all desirous of Sita's hand because in beauty she resembles Lakshmi, the beloved of Lord Vishnu.

Hence, bitten by humiliation, anger and arrogance those kings got united together and launched an attack upon my kingdom. They continued to besiege Mithila for one full year. Realizing the gravity of the situation, I sought the cooperation of my god-like friendly kings and routed them all. Thereafter the security of Mithila and this Shiva-bow was tightened."

"Maharaja! You have used the word 'brought-up daughter for Sita just now!"

"Janaka!" laughed Vishwamitra and said, "It's very difficult to escape from Lakshmana."

"Who wants to escape? Because where the saviour is, nobody knows." Janaka burst into peals of laughter and then as if lost in some sweet memory he said, "There is a tradition that a king has to plough the land symbolically for yajna. Years ago when I was doing this noble deed, I was told by my officials that an unknown newly born girl was found while the land was being tilled for yajna. At that time my whole attention was fixed on the front part of the plough. While cultivating the land I was thinking that the Mother Earth yields countless gems to us. Concentrating on Sita, I felt that this girl also has emerged from the earth and I gave her the name 'Sita'. I tried to find out her origin.

But it was decided that since I had given that unknown girl the name 'Sita' I regarded myself her father and then I brought her up as my daughter."

"Maharaja! I have never heard of such a revolutionary and pure-hearted person as you are. Even an ordinary householder thinks thousand times about caste and creed before doing such a deed."

"That's why he remains an ordinary person." Vishwamitra said,"If an ordinary land is tilled in an extraordinary way, only then we come to know how much fertile this ordinary-looking earth is."

"Now that vow of mine has become a matter of deep concern for me. If I had even a little knowledge that no kshatriya would be able to lift this bow, I would never have kept such a condition." It seemed Janaka was plunged in his deep worry. He said, "How can I fulfill the responsibility of a father? After all, the daughter is to be married off."

"Then what difficulty lies in it?" said Lakshmana in a simple, innocent way. He added," You are the king who welcomes new values and new thoughts. You can proclaim that since no suitable match has been found for Sita, the condition is being withdrawn."

"Your suggestion is beautiful and far-sighted. But it's not so simple to change it in Kshatriya society." Vishwamitra's voice remained unchanged.

"Excuse me, Maharaja! It's not so difficult also as you're thinking. Please consider this suggestion peacefully and seriously. I am sure that your heart and awakened intelligence will accept it as you are a setter of new values of life."

A messenger informed that Shiva-bow was going to reach its destined place. So they should all be ready for departure.

× × ×

A big chariot consisting of eight wheels was being pulled by hundreds of soldiers. There was a gigantic box in it. There were bowmen at all the four corners of that box. They were quite alert. They were turning their eyes all around so as to be ready to cope with an unexpected situation.

"Maharaja!"said Lakshmana, " I think eight or twelve horses can pull this huge chariot. Then why have so many soldiers been yoked to it?"

"Not yoked, Lakshmana!" Janaka smiled, "They themselves are pulling it. There is no reason behind it. It's only their devotion that is working behind it. They have boundless faith in Shiva-bow. If the chariot is being pulled by animals, the devotees of Shiva think that it is not only against Shiva's glory but also an insult to him. They believe that they themselves are animals and they are fortunate enough to be in the service of 'Pashupatinath' i.e. Shiva."

"Oh! Pardon me, Maharaja!" Lakshmana was stung by hesitation. "When I see any incident, the first feeling that arises in me is of extreme sensitiveness. I never pay my attention to this pious and spiritual side. When I looked at this scene from the view-point of rationality, a sort of curiosity was born in me. And now when I look at it from the view-point of devotion and spirituality, I experience a lot of peace and joy."

All were silent. They went on looking at the scene how all the soldiers and priests were pulling the chariot, then how they stopped to put down the box respectfully at its destined place.

"Maharaja! Is this bow taken out in a procession like this every time?"

"I don't understand what you want to say," Janaka looked at Lakshmana.

"Lakshmana! He wants to know why you are asking this question- it's purpose, do you understand?" Vishwamitra tried to pull his leg.

"O God!" Lakshmana beat his head and then spoke to Janaka, "Maharaja! I suffer from a malady that I want to ask something different. What I have to ask doesn't become evident from my question."

"It doesn't matter. Mould the language of your question again," laughed Janaka.

"I want to know that if any kshatriya comes tomorrow and say that he wants to see this bow or that he is excited to pull the string of the bow, will you then let it come out in a procession every day? This will incur a loss of too much time of the kingdom."

"It's a beautiful curiosity of yours, Son!" said Janaka. "Such kinds of arrangements are not made everyday. Some time ago when this kind of arrangement was made, the bow remained at the festival site for a certain period of time. When the contestants who arrived here failed in their attempt, it was restored to its place again. After that, nobody sent any proposal of this kind. Perhaps the entire kshatriya community has understood that in the present situation the earth is devoid of their glory and pride. They don't want to come to Mithila because they don't want to be the butt of others' mockery. They have found another beautiful reason to escape from it."

"What reason!" Lakshmana burst out.

"When Kshatriya princes, who could not come, saw the abortive attempts made by the kings greater than themselves, they began to say that it was a child's play for them to pull the string of the bow, but they couldn't even think of establishing their relations with Sita whose dynasty was unknown. It was the cover-up of their disability to pull the string of the bow."

"What a wonderful reason to hide their inefficiency!" said Lakshmana. "It would have been better if they had said that ordinary Kshatriyas like them had no strength even to touch the pious bow."

"It needs the purity of the heart to say so, Lakshmana!" said Janaka. "That's why I am saying that the earth is now devoid of chivalrous persons."

"But it is not right to say so in the presence of Shri Rama." It was a sudden outburst of Lakshmana's excitement and zeal.

"Son! Rama is an exception." Smilingly Janaka passed his hand on Lakshmana's head.

"Pardon me, Maharaja! What should I do for getting so deeply excited or instigated? " Lakshmana felt ashamed of himself.

The box opened on all four sides and in its middle was placed a grand and unique gigantic bow. As Rama saw it, again, he felt grateful to Vishwamitra. He began to think, "It is gurudeva's extreme grace upon me. I would never have seen such a beautiful, mighty and gigantic bow, perhaps. It's quite evident from its shape and size, and its metal that it must be very heavy. It has been built in such an artistic way that it doesn't appear to be a weapon of war. On the contrary, it looks as if it were a beautiful specimen of a thing of art."

"Rama! Look at this bow carefully. Will you be able to pull its string?" Asked Vishwamitra while looking at Rama.

On hearing what Vishwamitra said, all had their reactions depicted on their faces except Rama.

It was Janaka's heart that palpitated most, 'Why, I paid no attention to this. Lakshmana had already said clearly that I shouldn't proclaim that the earth was devoid of kshatriyas in the presence of Rama. Even then I didn't catch the hint. Perhaps it had settled in my mind that when so many kings and princes returned their home desperately, this work was impossible. This is the reason why I took the incident of showing the bow to Rama and Lakshmana at the instance of Vishwamitra a mere contextual happening. Was it already known to Rama and Lakshmana why they had come here? No, no, it can't be so; otherwise Vishwamitra would have already made it clear to me. I don't know what lies in their heart. But Vishwamitra has given me a ray of hope by putting forward this proposal before Rama. May Lord Shiva have his grace upon me so that I may not have to reconsider Lakshmana's suggestion.'

As if keeping his mind aside, Rama looked at the bow. He bowed his head before it with full devotion. On seeing this, Janaka felt ecstatic. He was happy to note that Rama was courteous as well as humble. No other kshatriya who came here up till now bowed his head before it. Intoxicated with their strength and power, they fell upon the bow as if it were a lifeless animal bound with a rope and as if they themselves were butchers. But as soon as they touched the bow, they felt electrified and were thrown afar. It seems that this Shiva-bow is active all the time, charged with electricity. It doesn't allow anyone to touch itself. Then the question of lifting it and pulling its string doesn't arise.

After bowing his head before the Shiva-bow, Rama touched the feet of Vishwamitra and said, "Gurudeva! Whatever has happened up till now, I've always found the might of guru's blessings in the background. For me the important thing is that I should obey you. If it is your ardent desire that I should pull the string of this grand Shiva-bow, I'll try, keeping in mind the image of Lord Shiva, to fulfill your desire."

'Oh, Rama! Who are you?' A thirsty wordless voice erupted from the depth of Janaka's heart. When Janaka's intelligence became active, he thought that it meant Vishwamitra hadn't told even Rama and Lakshmana what lay in his heart. Rama advanced towards the bow devotionlly.

A deep silence reigned in the whole premises. Before this, there had always been a great commotion at such a kind of function. Whenever anyone stepped forward to this bow, their servants, friends and relatives hailed him loudly in order to encourage him. But such a kind of silence and peace had never prevailed on an occasion of this type. There was a sort of secret joy on everyone's face.

Janaka wanted to see only this much whether an impossible task could be possible.

"Brother!"called out Lakshmana.

Rama looked towards him

"If you couldn't fulfill your promise?"

"Then I'll accept that Lord Shiva didn't consider me deserving."

"If you fulfilled your promise?"

"Then I'll be fortunate enough to be the medium of fulfilling gurudeva's desire."

"I am not saying that, brother! You will have to accept Sita as your wife,"it was a sort of warning from Lakshmana. It was quite clear from his words that Rama was taking an important decision of marrying Sita without father's permission.

"Lakshmana!" said Rama in his sweet voice," There's a clear-cut instruction from our father, Maharaja Dashratha, that I should give utmost importance to each and every order of gurudeva Vishwamitra. Then where is the scope of doubt?"

Lakshmana felt astonished and kept looking at Rama who stepped forward towards the bow.

When Rama approached the bow, he realized that it was not something lifeless but it was active because of some system which made it send out electric currents. These currents were wonderful in reading one's thoughts. So, naturally, when anyone attempted to touch it so as to pull its string, its currents would throw away the evil minded person. As Rama's left hand went on moving towards the middle part of the bow, he closed his eyes. He felt that he could see in the same way as with his open eyes. When there was hardly any distance left between the middle part of the bow and that of his palm, the bow, as if by some gravitational force, stuck to his palm. Rama gripped the bow gently with his fingers. Rama realized as if Lord Shiva himself were standing before him and saying, "Rama! Only a person like you who have congenial energy currents is allowed to launch this bow of mine. In future if this amazing bow is misused for some reason or the other or if someone comes to know how it was made, you should render it inactive before this. On getting the conducive energy, the bow will cooperate with you. Your desire itself will enable you to launch it. Holding its middle part firmly, you should pull its string and then order it to deactivate itself. Immediately after receiving your mental instruction, the suicidal explosive material used in its middle part will become active. Then along with terrible explosion, it will burst in such a way that nobody will be able to use it thereafter."

A question as if devoid of words arose within Rama, 'At present there is a gathering of people here. If the explosion harmed anyone, then...?'

Shiva's transparent image smiled again. Rama heard as if it were saying, 'No, there is a special characteristic of this suicidal explosion that it will produce only a terrible sound while destroying its inner build-up. It won't damage anything kept in the outside premises.'

Rama was quite familiar with this science of the bow, that is, after identifying energy currents, to get activated and launched by itself, and not harming others while destroying itself. It was a kind of living consciousness connected with warfare.

All the people present there were looking at Rama with astonishment. They were thinking that the Shiva-bow, instead of throwing Rama away, had clung to him and in what state bowing Rama is! Then all saw that Rama raised the bow carefully and conveniently. There was a strange kind of brightness on his face. His whole body was resplendent with attraction and joy, perhaps because of boundless energy.

Rama felt that as soon as he lifted the bow, electric currents became activated and formed a circle in the midst of the bow. He had never experienced such a kind of limitless source of energy. He felt as if the whole universe was insignificant before his might He pulled the bow's string and activated its suicidal explosives by means of his desire. There was an abrupt explosion of terrible nature in the silent campus. Rama experienced the horrible image of explosion. According to his conjecture, the impact of the sound of that terrible explosion could naturally damage all around. Rama noticed that Vishwamitra, Janaka and Lakshmana were standing smilingly as before, as if nothing happened. His eyes fell upon others too. They were all lying on the ground.

'What happened to them?'thought Rama for some moments. Rama continued to stand as before and waited for the final result of the bow's break. All the soldiers, servants and many other officials of the kingdom began to rise from the ground. It looked from their facial expressions that they had either become unconscious for a moment because of the impact of terrible sound or lay on the ground from security point of view, fearing damage and destruction.

In a short while, the entire premise echoed with the slogan "Victory to Rama! Victory to Rama! " By the gesture of his hand, Janaka instructed them all to be silent. He advanced towards Vishwamitra and said joyfully, "Gurudeva! Whatever has happened is beyond one's reasoning and thinking. It's an extremely wonderful incident. This animated bow never allowed any unwanted hand to touch it. It was kept as it is when my great ancestor, Devaraata had given it to me. The world has seen with its own eyes the chivalry and chastity of Shri Rama, the son of Dashratha."

The king's officials were collecting the scattered parts of the bow with astonishment. But now it was a lifeless object. They kept them at the same place. The bow's pieces looked like the collection of revered bones after the last rites of cremation.

"Gurudeva! My daughter Sita will definitely enhance the prestige and glory of my dynasty by choosing Dashratha's son, Rama as her husband." Janaka made a humble request," If you permit me, shall I send my courtiers by the fastest chariots with the good news to Maharaja Dashratha and invite him respectfully to Shri Rama 's marriage? Let me also send a message that both the sons of his are safe and sound in Mithila under your patronage."

"Amen!" Vishwamitra raised both of his hands happily by way of blessing.

" There's one curiosity in me, gurudeva!" Janaka's voice was doubt-ridden, "I hope Maharaja Dashratha will have no problem with this relation?"

Vishwamitra looked at Janaka. It appeared as if his eyes were saying," Hasn't Janaka heard what Rama said or has he no faith in Vishwamitra?"

It seemed as if Janaka had read Vishwamitra's eyes what they were saying. Before Vishwamitra could say anything, Janaka said," I am saying this thing only because no invitation was ever sent from Mithila to Ayodhya regarding Sita's marriage."

"Your doubt is weightless, Janaka!" There was sharpness in Vishwamitra's voice, "The first thing is that Sita has been declared to be an eligible girl for marriage for those who are really chivalrous. After this proclamation, there is no sense in sending a separate invitation card. Proclaimation, in itself, is an invitation. The entire Kshatriya clan was aware of your condition for marriage. It can't be possible that it is not known to Ayodhya. Those who spread rumours say many insignificant things. Some kshatriyas went to the extent of saying that if Janaka had been a real father of Sita, he would never have imposed such an evil condition. He is simply a father to her, her breeder. Hence he has done so intentionally."

Janaka was speechless. He was thinking why common people said anything they felt like without respecting anybody's feelings. They wished that Sita's husband would be a matchless person. God had not only kept his honour intact but also had given him unlimited renown. If that unimaginable event hadn't occurred, he would have reconsidered Lakshmana's proposal which was very dear to him.

"On hearing this news, Ayodhya will be puffed up with pride. It will spread like fire in all the three worlds- that it is Shri Rama, Ayodhya's Kshatriya prince, who has proved his chivalry by fulfilling Janaka's condition which no other Kshatriya had been successful in, and which had been a challenge to them and had forced them to bow their heads in shame. It is an ornament- like if a kshatriya is chosen by Sita.

"Gurudeva!" Janaka greeted him emotionally, "I am contented to hear this from your mouth, your arrival is here Lord Shiva-like."

* * *

9

Dashratha's chariot was ahead of all chariots. Guru Vashishtha was sitting beside him, lost in his own thoughts. Dashratha cast his looks upon other chariots coming behind. But he found an ocean of chariots and soldiers everywhere shorelessly. If it had been a war campaign, there would have been no music and no such attraction. But it was an organization of the wedding party to fetch the bride home, and so the instrumental music was being played on. There were many artists for entertainment. Many priests sitting in the chariot were performing yajna to purify the atmosphere. Its effect had made it fragrant and energy -providing. All were excited and happy. The wealth gifted by Janaka was indescribable. It seemed that if Sita had not been Janaka's brought-up daughter, he would perhaps not have gifted so much. But he left no stone unturned in providing that though he was a mere father to Sita, he made no partiality.

Dashratha's eyes fell upon guru Vashishtha. He was still sitting, lost in his happy thoughts. Dashratha wanted to unfold his heart now. He thought it unwise to refrain himself from doing so. He addressed Vashishtha in a happy tone, " Gurudeva!"

Vashishtha opened his eyes and said smilingly, "Dashratha! I hope you're happy."

"It's all your blessings, gurudeva!" Dashratha said in a very modest way, "I am suffering from a sense of guilt after expressing it before you as it is pricking me like a thorn. I'm sure I'll be free from that feeling of guilt after expressing it before you."

"Speak out," said Vashishtha as if it were an order.

"When Brahmrishi Vishwamitra demanded of me to send Rama to his ashrama to fight demons, I thought you had a golden chance to take revenge upon him for having insulted you and so I thought you would reject his proposal. I too would get an excuse not to send Rama with him without your consent. But when you gave your assent immediately, I had a rise of resentment in me for you. You to me....."

"Why did you stop? Let your thoughts and emotions come out of you. Don't stand as an obstacle in their way, otherwise you won't be able to free yourself from the sense of guilt." Vashishtha had understood what Dashratha wanted to say.

"Gurudeva! You seemed to me to be my killer and Rama's." There were tears in Dashratha's eyes, "Gurudeva! I'm really much distressed to feel that I had thought in a sinful manner about you. I wish to beg...."

"...to beg pardon of me is futile, Dashratha!"said Vashishtha softly. He added, "It is all human nature. It's a mendicant's nature to have no feeling of enmity for anyone. How can it be so with Vishwamitra? This kind of event is a part of man's life on account of the element of passion. You are competent enough to introspect yourself, O King! It is your sublime quality. You never hide anything. You're sinless or guiltless. You should, therefore, come out of your agony. Let's have some happy talk."

"Today Ayodhya is blessed with four brides. This is all your grace, Gurudeva! We were so much worried about Rama's marriage. And now Lakshmana has got Urmila as his wife. Bharata and Shatrughana have got Mandavi and Shrutkirti, the two daughters of Janaka's younger brother, Kushadhwaja." Dashratha thanked his stars for this and said further, "No doubt, Maharaja Janaka is a king but he has a high place amongst rishis and sages. He is definitely the only king on this earth, who is a mendicant also."

"He is discorporate," smiled Vashishtha. "He is the "Sidh" personage. He doesn't think himself to be a mere body. He constantly remembers that he is bodiless."

"God is great. He can make His appearance anywhere He likes. Nobody can understand His plans."

"How can one understand when He has no deliberate plan. He is beyond this all," said Vashishtha. He added, "And the most important thing is that it's not easy to know Him. Even if He is before you, you won't be able to know Him in the absence of divine eyes. You'll think that He is an ordinary being among men. If he is junior to you in rank or in relation, it becomes extremely difficult to accept and realize that within him God has emerged. Then a person is overpowered by vanity. It tells him that he is senior in age, in knowledge and in might. Then he begins to think how God can bless another person, and not the one who possesses so many virtues."

"Excuse me, gurudeva! How can it be that God makes His appearance and nobody is able to see and understand Him? It seems to me to be unreasonable. How can it be possible that if the sun rises, there is no light?"

"King!" Vashishtha looked at Dashratha kindly as if he were answering to an ignorant child. He said, "Life does not depend on reasons. It's a different thing that your reason matches with something in your life cycle. You say that it seems absurd if God emerges and nobody is able to see or hear him.Tell me one thing if you can hear those sounds which can be heard by beasts."

"No."

"When ordinary insects, birds and beasts can see sights and hear those sounds which you can't, how can you say so about God? He is present all the time but competency is also needed to see Him. You say that if the sun rises, how can it be possible that there is no light! No, it isn't possible. Here you are right."

Vashishtha looked at Dashratha smilingly like a hunter and said, "But it is possible that the sun rises and vanity clouds your eyes resulting in darkness before you or if you become sightless, the sun and the light will be useless for you, or you close all the doors of your mental eye or take shelter in the dark cave. This thing is at least possible. O King! Then in such a situation what light will do?"

Dashratha became unanswerable. He kept on looking at Vasishtha.

"O King! If I say Rama, your son Shri Ramachandra, has the image of God or he is God Himself who is born in your family as your son, what will you say?" asked Vasishthta in his mysterious voice.

"Gurudeva! Rama is only a child. Even those saints and sages who sat in meditation for ages together could not get Him, where does Rama stand? He has not even full knowledge of the world, then to achieve God..."

"I'm not talking about achieving Him. I'm simply saying that it is He who is born in your house", smiled Vashishtha.

Dashratha laughed wildly and said, "I'll always remember today's interesting talk of yours, gurudeva!... and then who is Dashratha? Father of the Supreme Power God!"

Dashratha's laughter knew no bounds. When the intensity of his laughter reduced, he said, "Gurudeva! Only Kshtriyas are born in a royal family. Why will that unborn God appear in a kingly family?"

Vashishtha said nothing. He had his eyes upon the sky. Kites and other birds were flying in the sky. Their horrible sound was coming down nearer. On their right hand a pack of deer was running. There was a queer kind of peace in the atmosphere.

"Gurudeva! These birds are hovering and making a noise; it's an inauspicious sign. But since the deer are running on our right, it's an auspicious sign. What does it mean when both sign of opposite nature are together?" There was a tinge of anxiety in Dashratha's voice.

"O King! It's clear that an unhealthy sign will be swept away by a healthy one" laughed Vashishtha.

Vashishtha's laughter frightened Dashratha. He began to think, "This is the greatest problem with spiritual people that they always talk mysteriously."

"How will inauspicious thing occur and how the auspicious one?" Dashratha wanted to get it clarified. "In what form will the unhealthy sign be?"

"Why didn't you ask about the auspicious thing? It would have been better if you had said that there was nothing to worry about in case of inauspicious thing being swept away by the auspicious one. The matter ends here itself..." said Vashishtha.

"Gurudeva! You're on a high pedestal of life where profit and loss, weal and woe, auspicious and inauspicious have no meaning. But we people are ordinary householders living under the influence of illusion. We always remain scared of evil things. In our life the shadow of woe always accompanies the moments of happiness, and it consumes our momentary joy like 'Rahu'", said Dashratha frightenedly.

"Don't be scared, O King! It's a signal for furious sandstorm to blow. Look, the horizon is being covered by the storm. It will blow and disappear. No harm will come, only that some people's hearts will quiver", said Vashishtha.

Dashratha looked towards the sky", "Oh! It's only an ordinary storm which is possible to blow...and I was unnecessarily doubt-ridden. Like the stream of water gushing out after the breach of a dam, the furious storm came suddenly. It brought with it a swarm of dust, pebbles and dry leaves. Even horses were finding it difficult to hold the ground. The flags fitted in chariots seemed to be trembling. The noise created by the storm was terrible. It looked as if the god of wind would take away everything with it. The foot soldiers hid behind the chariots. Whosoever got any place, took shelter there.

Dashratha folded his hands and began to pray to God to let the storm pass away. He saw Vashishtha sitting in the chariot with his closed eyes as if it were not a storm but a boat journey on the full moon day.

The storm that came with full fury disappeared with the same speed. It was like a pack of wild buffaloes that destroys everything on its way while stampeding.

When everything became normal, the charioteer drove the chariot farther. Hardly had they gone a little distance when they seemed to see a troop of soldiers well-equipped with weapons. They looked neither demons nor soldiers but mendicants who had tied their long entwined hair on the back. They had long beards. Each of them was wearing a string of beads (rudraksh) on arms, round the neck and on head. Besides these, each had a bow and an axe. A gigantic armed sage was standing aloof from them. It looked as if other armed mendicants were his reflection.

"Rama and here!" Vashishtha stood up and got down from the chariot. He advanced towards him.

"Rama! He called out gleefully."

"Where is Rama, gurudeva! It's Parashurama now - the bitter enemy of Kshatriyas. It seems that even the sandstorm was running away from him. Now we have fallen in his way. God knows what charges of atrocity and injustice he puts upon us and then he fights."

"Dashratha greets you, Lord Parashurama!" Dashratha in his most modest way admired Parashurama many times and in many ways.

Parashurama's heaving got reduced. His face was telling them that he was in great rage. But since Vashishtha was there and Dashratha behaved most devotionally, his anger subsided like the milk that rises but subsides when it is splashed with cold water.

"Dashratha, where is your son, Rama?" asked Parashurama. He neither blessed him nor uttered any word of formality.

Dashratha's heart palpitated hard as if it were saying, 'Only this inauspicious thing remained behind. And gurudeva was saying that it would be swept away by the auspicious one. Now Parashurama will not spare anyone alive. God knows who has poisoned his mind against Rama and now, without knowing any reason, he will punish Rama, my son. He has such bitter enmity with Kshatriyas that without hearing what they want to say he declares his verdict.'

"Rama stands before you, Lord! Accept my greetings."

Dashratha turned his head behind and saw Rama standing. He got stunned. He didn't know why Rama got down from his chariot to come over here. After all, he and guru Vashishtha were there. They themselves could have appeased Parashurama. It was quite certain that since guru Vashishtha was present, Parashurama would not indulge in killing anyone. But the presence of Rama had added fuel to the fire.

"What do you think of yourself, Rama?" Parashurama exploded like a volcano. "Your name is nothing but another form of my name. However, in behaviour you're the part of the same arrogant Kshatriya society."

Rama gazed at Parashurama pleasantly.

'Oh, this Rama is instigating him to raise his weapon against him instead of falling at his feet and begging him to pardon him if he has done anything wrong involuntarily.'

"Lord!" said Dashratha in his trembling voice.

"Keep quiet, Dashratha!" said Parashurama angrily. He turned towards Rama, "Why are you looking at me so?"

"Lord! I see that in spite of being a Brahmin you're an image of burning rage. How will an ordinary person pick up idealism to gain victory over his weakness? To have divine glory and to be furious are two different states." Rama's looks seemed to be piercing Parashuram.

When Dashratha noticed this, he couldn't understand how Rama was so full of passionate zeal. 'Has he lost his senses? Doesn't he know that he is challenging Parashuram?' thought Dashratha.

Parashuram had never expected such a kind of answer from Rama. He had assumed that both father and son would fall at his feet and cry. Then he would go away after giving them simple punishment, keeping in mind guru Vashishtha's honour. But here it was...

"Rama!" Parashuram wanted to give a boost to his fury within him and express it by means of his voice. But he felt as if someone was throwing water on the burning pieces of coal. "Don't you know that I have shed the blood of kshatriyas on this earth?"

"This is only your illusion, lord!" Rama's animated voice echoed, "Think it over again and then say. Have you shed the blood of kshatriyas or of cruel persons on this earth? A cruel man has only one caste - and it is that he is a demon. If any Kshatriya or Vaishya or even a Brahmin is cruel, he will be called a demon."

'Rama! You don't know that you've used the wrong word 'demon' for Parashuram.' Dashratha was trembling from within and one could notice the signs of fear on his body.

"I know that an unjust and unwise animal- like person had killed your great and chaste-hearted father. Accidentally, he was born in a kshatriya family. But many years ago he was out of kshatriya clan because of his wicked deeds and then he joined the group of demons. But you didn't notice this change. A real kshatriya is the one who sacrifices his life for the protection of cows, brahmins and women. Don't you think you are promoting the cause of demons by killing such kshatriyas? The element of truth loses its lustre before the fire of anger, lord! Come out of the garb of personal enmity and think it over. Then say whether you would like to kill a kshatriya who is just and duty-bound."

Parashuram had no answers to it. He kept on looking at Rama. He was trying to discover anger within himself. But Rama's voice and his divinity pacified him. It was the same feeling of calmness which he used to experience when he was lost in his state of meditation.

"Rama is your devotee. He feels enchanted by your divine glory." There was pleasure and pride in Rama's voice. He added, "I've seen in you a wonderful kind of confidence of a sage and kshatriya. When a kshatriya goes out of his bounds, a brahmin should empower himself to maintain balance on the earth. This is what you've done. You've faith in justice, truth and non-violence. But you adopted violence to deal with the crisis. I'm really grateful to you for this divine device."

"I've heard you've destroyed Shiva-bow, 'Ajagava'." There was accusation in Parashuram's voice.

"What you've heard is true, lord!" Rama folded his hands and said, "I did this only after getting gurudeva Vishwamitra's consent, and also to fulfil Maharaja Janaka's desire."

"But the condition was only to pull the string of the bow", Parashuram reasoned.

"What you're saying is true, lord!" Lakshmana felt that he would no longer be able to contain himself. A naughty child sitting within him came out and said, "But that bow itself had told brother Rama to liberate itself from that life of old age."

Parashuram looked at Lakshmana angrily.

"Lakshmana!" Rama raised his left hand in the direction of Lakshmana without looking at him. It was a clear instruction that he should not interrupt.

Lakshmana looked at Parashuram smilingly. His eyes were telling him that he was silent only because of his brother, otherwise...

"The bow itself had instructed me to destroy it. I realised that Lord Shiva sitting in meditation was instructing me to do so. But I can't give you any proof of it or any plea. My words themselves are its proof."

"No, Rama! You'll have to give its proof, come what may. And I have a device to judge whether it is true or not." It looked as if Parashuram was searching for something in Rama. He said, "I can't make myself believe that you lifted Shiva bow. The question of destroying it comes later."

"Tell me what favourite work of yours I can do to give a proof of what I've said. I'm ready for test."

"I challenge you for a duel", said Parashuram and he removed the wonderful bow suspending from his shoulder.

Dashratha felt like screaming and say, 'This is all injustice. If you fight a boy with your divine weapon, his death is certain.'

But before Dashratha could say anything, Rama spoke, "If this challenge had been given to him by a kshatriya, I would have honoured it. But I've said just now that a kshatriya does not kill a cow, a brahmin and a woman. He thinks it is illegal and unjust. You're a brahmin. You're worthy of our worship, not for fight."

Parashuram looked at Rama mysteriously and said, "Rama! Do you know that the bow which you destroyed belonged to Lord Shiva and the bow which I have belongs to Lord Vishnu. When both of them were made, there was a war between Lord Shiva and Lord Vishnu to test it. The Shiva-bow was defeated by the Vishnu-bow. Now you can understand the might and greatness of this bow. If the entire kshatriya clan is terribly scared of me, it's not for nothing. They know that my weapon is sufficient enough to kill them. And if I make use of this bow, it will cause complete devastation."

Parashuram paused for a while, looked at Rama and then said, "Nobody else but me and Lord Vishnu can even touch this bow. If you are able to pull its string and release arrow from it, I'll be satisfied."

"Definitely! But if a kshatriya pulls the string of any bow, you know very well what it means." There was determination in Rama's voice.

Parashuram batted his eyelashes and nodded his head by way of giving his consent.

Rama looked at the bow lovingly. He greeted it and took it from Parashuram's hands as if it were some fruit. Rama gazed at Parashuram with boundless smile and pulled its string. It was adorned with an arrow.

Tears of joy gushed out of Parashuram's eyes. He could clearly see that it was Lord Vishnu standing before him with his matchless smile.

Dashratha couldn't understand what this was all happening. What did Parashuram see in Rama that he was so overwhelmed with emotions? This behaviour of his, it seemed, had damaged his image of anger for which he was so well-known.

Parashuram realised that Lord Vishnu's might within him had gone out and established itself in Rama.

"I've satisfied you. Now you give me a word that you'll leave for Mahendra mountain for ever. Now Rama is here to establish religion on earth."

"I'm not only satisfied but also contented, lord!" Parashuram greeted Rama and said, "Now I've no work here when you are present."

Dashratha was astonished to see what had happened to Parashuram. He is saying 'Lord' to Rama. He couldn't understand anything. He could only see his brave son, Rama, who was smiling.

* * *

10

It was evening. The Sun-god was stepping down the steps of red-hued clouds and going down into the underworld pool. In the opposite direction the moon was rising smilingly. The flock of birds was returning to its nests in one file. The terrace of the palace was adorned with creepers and plants bearing different kinds of flowers. Rama was lost in the evening's beauty. He was reclining in a swing. His eyes were feasting upon natural beauty. He closed his eyes in a way as if he were sipping some sweet drink slowly and enjoying its every draught. Then a sweet smile played on his lips.

Taking Rama's hands in her soft hands, she pushed the bed-like swing at regular intervals. She was gazing at Rama amorously, enjoying Rama's pleasing smile.

"Rama!" Sita addressed Rama in her musical voice as if it were the sound of Veena, a musical instrument.

"Hmm!" Rama looked at Sita. Smilingly, he put around Sita's neck one of the garlands gently.

"Oh Rama!" A wave of joy ran through Sita's whole body. "In your company time flies."

"Why don't you look at those birds that are flying in the sky? These are different kinds of birds, twittering different notes. They are filled with extreme joy. How excited they're to return to their nests after the whole day long weal and woe! Aren't you enjoying this natural beauty?" Rama cooperated with Sita by clapping his hands.

"I'm noticing all this, my lord! But it's all through your eyes. When I look at a scene without peeping into your eyes, I find no music and no animation in that." Sita passed her hands lovingly over Rama's long hair.

"Seetey!" called Rama.

"Hmm...."

"Don't you feel that you're love-bitten?

"How?" Sita sat up in her jovial mood. It indicated that Rama's inner feelings were no longer buried within him. It meant that he was ready to converse with her.

"Why don't you take your food before I return?"

"Didn't I say that everything without you is tasteless? But when you are with me, food becomes palatable. Whenever you get late, my cousins try to persuade me many times to take food, but it never goes down my throat. So far as breakfast is concerned, somehow or the other I manage to take it. But your company is essential when I take morning and evening meals."

"This is what I'm saying, Seetey that many times I return after mid-night when I am engaged in performing state duties. In such a situation, if you have your food, I'll feel very happy. I understand your feelings, but..."

"Leave aside your 'but' and answer one question of mine. 'Why don't you say that you take your food outside when you get late?' Don't you try to take your food when I'm sitting before you?"

"Well, I give you one more reason for this", laughed Rama.

"It means that you've accepted your defeat in case of the first matter."

"Yes, my love!" Rama dramatically bowed his head.

"I'm happy, Rama!" Sita lapsed into her childlike laughter. She added, "Now you can present your second reason.

"As you command , my love!" said Rama. He added, "You make our mothers the source of your inspiration. They all take the delicious and tasty food in the absence of Maharaja Dashratha. But it doesn't mean that they have less love for him."

Sita said nothing.

"You didn't answer me?"

Sita still remained silent.

Rama looked at Sita. Tears were flowing from Sita's eyes. Her eyes were getting red.

"I don't mean to say that you love me less or you simply make a fake demonstration of it. Oh, Seetey! I am only joking." It was quite clear from Rama's voice that he himself felt hurt when he saw Sita hurt. He was overbrimmed with love for Sita. He realised that he shouldn't have harassed Sita even out of joke.

"It is not so, Aryaputra!" Sita wiped her tears and said, "After some time you'll become Ayodhya's king..."

"And after becoming the king, I'll have scarcity of time. Then you'll have to wait for a longer time. I suppose this is the cause of your anxiety!" Rama wished to change the whole atmosphere into a light vein.

"No, my lord!"

"Then!"

"After your becoming the king of Ayodhya, the kings of other countries would like to establish sweet and friendly relations with a prosperous and powerful kingdom like Ayodhya. Some countries will take a step ahead of this. They would like to have family realtions with Ayodhya. The most common customary practice among kshatriyas is that a less powerful king is ever ready to give his daughter or sister in marriage to the king. As a result, polygamy is in practice. Many kings would wish to see that you marry more than once. Your councillors and courtiers will definitely give their approval to it saying that it lies in the interest of Ayodhya. The country with which nuptial relations are established can't afford to be an enemy of that country."

"If one adopts the strategy of marriage for sweet and happy relations, I think it is the most disgraceful commercial enterprise. There should be no place for any lust or treaties at the root of marriage. I accept marriage only if it is the epicentre of love. If there is no love in it, it is only a burden. Marriage has its beautiful and happy connection only with love." Each and every word of Rama was a reflection of his philosophy of life.

"Seetey! Nourish no doubt in your mind. Except for you, no other woman will ever be in Rama's mind. This is Rama's solemn promise. I take you to be my better-half, not a wife."

"If it's a political compulsion, then...?"

"Maharaja Dashratha will never issue such a decree that goes against my promise. He knows its implication fully well."

"And mothers?"

"You are so dear to them that they can never think of anyone else. Then they are conversant with practical difficulties arising from polygamy. They themselves don't feel tempted to have more wives for their sons."

"Oh Rama! You've lightened me of my burden."

"Victory to Shri Ramachandraji!" Lakshmana's voice echoed.

"See, Lakshmanaji has come. The naughty child enshrined in his heart is always active. He will either laugh himself and make others laugh or get angry and make others weep." Sita's voice was a reflection of her boundless affection and pride for Lakshmana.

Lakshmana was being accompanied by Bharata and Shatrughana. Their wives were following them. They all entered and greeted Rama and Sita respectfully. Rama blessed them all by kissing and Sita embraced Urmila, Mandavi and Shrutakirti.

"Perhaps some serious discussion was going on", said Lakshmana jokingly.

"Yes, Lakshmana! Sita was praising you for your great qualities", Rama teased Lakshmana.

"But it seemed from sister-in-law's eyes that you were using some severe words for her," said Shatrughana in his low voice. He succeeded in conveying to all what he wanted to say.

"I've one question to ask", said Sita in a simple, pleasing way.

"Aha! I'm in deep love with questions. As a matter of fact, the question mark itself is close to my heart. If questions are there, we'll try to seek their answers. If we do so, solutions to the problems will be before us. If solutions are there, then..."

"...Even then you won't remain silent." Shatrughana cut Lakshmana in and said, "Will you listen to the sister-in-law or continue to harp on your things?"

"Oh, this servant begs your pardon!" bowed Lakshmana his head in a dramatic way.

"If a king declares that his daughter will marry that kshatriya who fulfils his promise of deactivating the bow, what will you all do in such a situation?"

"All of us have unshaken faith in being devoted to one wife only. Therefore, no such proposal or invitation is acceptable to us," Bharata said in a courteous way. He added, "Such a kind of baseless feeling can never arise in our heart."

"Bharata brother!" spoke out Lakshmana.

"Speak, Lakshmana!"

"Will you ever bid good-bye to your seriousness and bindings? First, you always keep quiet. If you ever open your mouth, you start preaching. Sometimes you should answer in a comical way too!"

"How can there be any comical answer to this serious question?" said Bharata in a light vein. He added, "Answers to all deep questions are also deep. What answer will you give to this question?"

"Its first, simple and easy answer is that we are all devoted to one wife only. Therefore, we find ourselves incompetent to take part in this competition. There is no question of such an anxiety as our father Maharaja Dashratha has taken no such vow."

As Lakshmana said so, all burst into laughter producing the tinkling sound like that of gold coins falling upon the hard ground. Only Rama was smiling sweetly.

"And what can be its second answer?"

Mandavi's laughter knew no pause.

"Its second answer is that now there is no such bow left as mighty as Shiva-bow. Therefore, even if an invitation comes to us to participate in the competition it will be followed by the message that Ayodhya's princes should take no trouble in coming over here. It is because all the kings have destroyed that bow with their cumulative efforts. Now the question before us is that whom our single daughter should marry. We have put ourselves into trouble by imitating Maharaja Janaka. May God save us! May God save us!!"

This time even Rama couldn't help laughing. When Rama stopped laughing, Urmila said, "We have come here with one mission in our mind."

The men-servants and maid-servants came here with light meal. Sita told them to place the food-stuff at its appropriate place. She served it and all her cousins helped her in doing so. At the mere gesture of Sita, all the skilled servants slipped away after rendering the necessary service.

"Yes, now Urmi, speak out,"going to the swing to sit on, Sita said. She put forward a plate of fruit and sweets before Rama.

"After some days, our marriage will complete one year", said Urmila.

"One year!" There was an element of surprise in Sita's voice. She added, "It seems to me as if we got married only yesterday itself."

"Now speak out!" Lakshmana clapped in order to attract everybody's attention towards himself. He said further, "What had I said that our Sita Ma would say this, and this is what she says."

"My dear Sir!" Will you keep quiet?" said Shrutakirti.

"No."

"Why?"

"Because keeping quiet is the nature of our brother, Bharata."

Again laughter echoed.

"Lakshmana! Until Urmila completes her statement, you'll keep quiet", There was an instruction in Sita's voice, but she was finding it difficult to control her laughter.

"As you order!" Lakshmana placed a finger upon his mouth.

"We all want to celebrate this occasion for three days. We'll have boating and an excursion into the forest in the lap of nature. In this connection we seek your wish and permission."

"Urmi! All of you have said what I had in my heart", Sita looked towards Rama and said, "Aryaputra!"

By way of acceptance, Rama smiled.

"Bharata! Shatrughana!" said Rama, "Did you consider the memorandum submitted by the representatives of the farmers of western zone?"

"Aryaputra! You discuss state matters. We're going back to our chambers." Sita stood up from her swing. She was followed by Urmila, Mandavi and Shrutakirti.

"Now you all go back to your chambers and leave us alone here. That's why Shri Rama has started discussion," said Lakshmana.

"Lakshmana!" Sita smiled, looking towards Lakshmana.

"It's only after the completion of Urmi's talk, I've broken my silence," Lakshmana gave his explanation.

"It's all right, you're pardoned!" said Urmila, teasing Lakshmana.

All the sisters left for their chambers.

"Farmers plead that this time their crops aren't good on account of some malady. In such a situation if the state reduces their tax, they will be very grateful." Shatrughana said, "The assistance sought by gurukulas has already been sent to them according to your instructions."

"What do both of you say about the farmers' trouble?"

"After investigating the matter, we've come to know that insects of some new species have destroyed the crops.

Geologists have found out its solutions. Most probably next year they will have very good crops in that area."

"After evaluating their condition correctly, a special concession should be given to the farmers, Bharata!" instructed Rama.

"Yes!" Bharata bowed his head.

"Brother!" said Shatrughana, "There was a discussion about state tax in one of the conferences of courtiers/ ministers from different countries. We were also present there along with Sumantraji. It was the opinion of majority of ministers that there would be a great loss to the public exchequer if concession was granted like this. Hence this sort of concession is useless."

"If the people live in woes, it's a great loss to the state. The true implication of royal treasury is that the state should speak its revenue on the upbringing of its people without any prejudice. Politics is not a commercial transaction but a beautiful system of running a family. Unless and until the state looks upon the people as the members of one family, there can't be any possibility of a happy nation," said Rama. He added, "A king should tax his people only that much which is required for their welfare. Let us take the case of a bumble-bee that sucks a flower only in a sustainable way. It never destroys it but makes it happy. After this, the flower's beauty increases."

"Although you are the son of Maharaja Dashratha yet the public looks upon you as if you were their father." Shatrughana said further, "Your orders will be carried out."

"Be happy and sensitive to the needs of the people. You should always be ready to work for their welfare ", saying so, Rama extended his large arms.

All three brothers shrank in his arms.

"Brother!" Bharata took Rama's hands in his hands and placed them on his forehead.

"Speak out, Bharata, what's the matter?" Rama passed his hands on Bharata's hand lovingly. Shatrughana and Laxmana fixed their looks upon Bharata.

"Yesterday father called me to say that our maternal uncle had been staying here for many days and now he wanted to go back to Kekaya country. At that time uncle was also there. He said, "Maharaja! I'll take Bharata with me."

Father said laughingly, "I knew this. But why did you take so many days to say this?"

"Then what did father say?" asked Shatrughana.

"What did father say?" Lakshmana looked at Shatrughana questioningly.

"Oh! What did the maternal uncle say?" Shatrughana realised his mistake.

"He gave a beautiful reply." He said, "Maharaja! They're so many things in life that are naturally understood.

Beauty lies in being silent. But when nobody understands its sound, one has to take refuge in words. It would have been better if Maharaja Dashratha had said, 'Brave Yudhajit! You're returning to Kekya. Tell me when you'll send back Bharata.'"

"After all, what does it mean? The maternal uncle is prejudicial in his behaviour. He talks only of Bharata to take with him, and no mention of my name", said Shatrughana complainingly.

"Shatrughana!" said Rama, "Pay attention to what the maternal uncle said. What a wonderful and quizzical thing he has said that there are many things in life that are naturally understood and that beauty lies in being silent! Whenever there is a talk about Bharata, you're naturally taken in."

"And when there is a talk about our respected brother Shri Ramachandraji, we three are already included in it", Bharata gave an affectionate slap on Shatrughana's cheek.

It seemed that Shatrughana felt ashamed of what he had said.

"What was the need for making the maternal uncle wait for so many days? You could have gone with him before this", said Lakshmana.

"The maternal uncle had told me so but brother Rama had assigned me some state work which I hadn't then completed," said Bharata. He added, "Now I have completed all that work. If....", Bharata looked towards Rama and said, "If I get your permission, only then I can go with him."

"... permission granted, Bharata! Go and enjoy yourself and make others happy in grandfather's house. I'm happy that you're the apple of everybody's eyes there," Rama embraced both Bharata and Shatrughana.

"We are the apple of your eyes also," said Bharata. His voice indicated that he was getting emotional.

"Bharata!" Rama gazed at him and said, "I feel your deep love for me. Don't be so over-emotional."

"Otherwise Mandavi sister-in-law will say that whenever Bharata returns from Rama after meeting him, he is seen weeping," said Lakshmana with his slanting eyes.

Bharata wiped out his eyes smilingly.

* * *

11

There was an inaugural ceremony of a new gurukula in Ayodhya. This gurukula was meant for the children of the royal family and of many other chief state authorities. The previous one was too small. When the head Acharya of the gurukula made his first appeal to Dashratha, the latter paid no attention to it. At the second request, he assured him that he would take his decision regarding this matter soon in future. The third time, the head Acharya made a request to Rama. Rama said, "Why did you take so much time in expressing such an important issue?" The head Acharya said, "I had already made my requests to Maharaja Dashratha twice." Rama said, "The Maharaja might have forgotten about it for being busy with other state matters. He no longer looks after education, army and finance." Within a year Rama got more beautiful and more gigantic gurukula built than what had been expected by the head Acharya. The head with his acharyas welcomed Dashratha. He was the chief guest on this occasion.

"Respected Head Acharya! You have invited all to this ceremony. But you haven't made it clear who will inaugurate this gurukula."

"Maharaja! I've kept it secret. When all the great personalities are present on the dais, I'll declare his name. We're fortunate enough to enjoy so much freedom under your patronage. Talent fully blossoms in your kingdom." There was a flavour of cordial respect in head acharya's voice.

"Shri Rama took no time in fulfilling all the possible requirements of gurukula, and that too without being asked for. It seems as if God Himself were supervising the construction work of the gurukula and giving His active contribution to it", said an acharya excitedly.

All the acharyas and the head Acharya present at that time were praising the administration of Ayodhya in different contexts. Dashratha was overjoyed when he heard this.

A large assembly of people had converged at the ceremony site. Even common people had been invited to this ceremony today so that they might also share food along with others. The chariots of royal officials could be seen far and wide. The horses yoked to chariots were decorated, gigantic and powerful. Charioteers were passing their hands on them affectionately. Beautiful flower designs and colourful flags in the gurukula were intensifying its beauty and attraction. There was an atmosphere of zeal and zest all around. Everyone looked jovial. Many people had arrived to see all the royal members gathered on this occasion.

The dais was huge and adequately high from all standards. Everybody could see and hear the great persons seated on the dais quite easily.

In the midst was sitting Maharaja Dashratha. Besides him was sitting guru Vasishtha clad in white clothes. He had white hair and white beard. Then Rama was sitting. Lakshmana was standing behind Rama. He was discussing certain things with those who had arranged this ceremony. On the left of Dashratha, representatives of neighbouring countries and very important courtiers and priests of Ayodhya were sitting. The head acharya's seat was beside Rama's. But he was moving on the dais here and there, giving instructions to all acharyas concerned before the start of the programme.

The head Acharya arose to speak on 'Vyaspeetha'. The conch echoed and deep silence established itself there. The head Acharya said in his resonant voice, "My hearty greetings to all the well-cultured people of Ayodhya kingdom that is equipped with all amenities of life and is more beautiful than heaven itself? My bowings to all great persons seated on the dais! What's more important than my statement is that you will see all this with your own eyes. You can see this beautiful ashrama, well-equipped with all educational facilities that was built in a short space of time. It's like a dream that has come true in an over-night. It seems that Shri Rama has himself blessed it like Vishwakarma, the architect of heaven."

The entire assembly of people was ecstatic at the mere mention of Rama. Many people began to dance out of joy. Clapping their hands, some began to sing 'Shri Rama, Our Rama'. Some others had brought with them their musical instruments and they expressed their joy by playing upon them.

This was the first opportunity in Dashratha's life when he was accompanied by Rama at such a grand ceremony. He recollected that when he himself was a crown Prince and whenever he accompanied his father at this type of grand ceremonies, he had neither seen nor heard the crown Prince being greeted with so much zeal by the public. And Rama was not yet a crown prince. It seemed that Dashratha had lost his own identity as the king of kings in the midst of eulogy showered upon Prince Rama.

Again, the conch sounded. The entire assembly of people burst into cries of joy. The moment the conch blower was ready to blow his conch, the head Acharya silenced him in a happy mood. He folded his hands and requested them to maintain silence. After a short while, silence again reigned there.

"I understand your feelings. But if you make so much happy noise at the mere mention of Shri Rama, how will I be able to enhance your joy by describing his divine qualities. I, therefore, request you all with my folded hands to remain silent so that I may share with you whatever I know about Rama."

The head Acharya began to mention Rama's virtues, "I still remember the very first day when I came to Rama with an appeal for the set up of gurukala. As I met him, I said, 'The most renowned and the best of men Prince Shri Rama, the son of Maharaja Dashratha ...'. On hearing this, Rama folded his hands and in the most humble way said to me, 'Great Acharya! What crime has this slave of yours committed that obliges you to hit me with your word-arrows? I am like your son, besides your pupil. You simply call me 'Rama'. There should be a feeling of authority in your voice, not that of a supplicant.' Friends!" the head acharya felt choked. Tears gushed out of his eyes. He burst into tears like a small child. If Lakshamana had not run to compose him, he would perhaps have lost his balance and fallen upon the dais. Lakshmana helped him drink some water from a small jug of water kept in a platter held by a Brahmchari standing nearby. Then he assured Lakshamana that he was all right and again continued to speak.

Even Lakshamana's eyes were full of tears. He saw how the entire gathering of people was wiping tears to have a clear image of Rama.

The head of gurukul continued mentioning Rama's qualities for long. Many things were thought to be unnatural for Dashratha. While describing Rama's qualities, the head acharya was putting Rama at par with God. In the whole context no mention of Dashratha was made. The king was astonished to note that the people of his kingdom were listening as if enchanted by some magic spell. He knew that people generally would become restless and get tired after listening to the description of a king or any royal personage for a little while. They leave the ceremony behind. But here it is not so. Even if the head Acharya is saying all this out of courtesy, who has charmed the public?' thought Dashratha.

'You're jealous of Rama's popularity or your vanity has possessed you wholly,' laughed Dashratha's inner voice.

Dashratha felt as if someone had used an ill-word for him. He felt embarrassed, 'Why should I be envious of him?'

'If it's not envy, why do you suffer from pain?' laughed the inner voice.

Dashratha thought that if his inner voice had a body, he would have chopped its head with his sword there and then itself.

'This is not my pain, but my estimation,' Dashratha ground his teeth.

'And the same is burning you to ashes. It has increased the rate of your breath and blood pressure. Why do you forget that if Rama is held in high esteem, you'll be able to hold your head higher. Why did you come down to Rama's appraisal as you heard his praise. Why didn't a fountain of joy play within you? Why didn't you dance out of joy? But alas! Your vanity blocked the stream of joy', chided Dashratha's voice.

Dashratha was speechless. He felt ashamed of himself and bent his head. Seeing this, the inner voice vanished. Dashratha put aside his haughtiness and looked at Rama. The head acharya was still motivating the young people with his description of Rama's personality and achievements. But Rama showed no reaction to it. He was sitting quite indifferent to his praises or that he was sitting on such a high pedestal that the words of praise didn't reach upto him.

But if Dashratha had been in place of Rama, he would have been flying on the wings of joy in the sky: He would have shown it on his face, but Rama....no.

"In the end, I've nothing else to say about who will inaugurate the new gurukula." As these words were uttered by the head Acharya, the public burst out joyfully, "Rama! Rama! Rama! Our Rama! Jai Shri Rama!"

As Dashratha heard this slogan, his heart was full of extreme joy. He thanked his inner voice for having pulled him from hell and pushed him into the region of ecstasy.

Rama rose up and came to Vyaspeetha. He touched the feet of the head Acharya and said, "All the people of Ayodhya! My heart and soul!"

Rama's address to the people in this manner filled the entire atmosphere with glee and cheerfulness. Rama silenced them all and said, "If any painting or a statue is extremely beautiful, its credit goes to the painter or sculptor. If sweet sound comes from a flute, the flute is not to feel proud of it. I'm simply a flute made of hollow bamboo. Through this medium the gurus and Maharaja Dashratha are singing songs of praise which you're listening with great attention."

Dashratha's eyes were filled with tears. At once he wiped them off. Dashratha looked towards guru Vasishtha who was already noticing Dashratha. Dashratha felt embarrassed. Vasishtha spoke to him in a low voice, "O King! Whether tears flow out of sorrow or joy, let them come out. Don't be a hurdle in their way."

Dashratha smiled at this. He thought that perhaps gurudeva Vasishtha knew the science of reading one's feelings.

"Rama's welfare lies hidden in the public welfare. I'm only a representative of Maharaja Dashratha, and in that capacity I've a right to serve. This is my duty as well. It's only Guru Vasishtha who will inaugurate the new gurukula and therein lies the pride of Ayodhya. I request the head Acharya to pray to Maharaja Dashratha, the chief guest on this occasion, that he should request Guru Vasishtha to inaugurate this new pious venture."

Again, the whole atmosphere echoed with joyous slogan.

*   *   *

Today Dashratha didn't go to any queen. He wished to stay in isolation. He came out of his chamber. While standing in his balcony, he was noticing how night had enveloped Ayodhya city. The roads were illuminated with light. People either in their chariots or on horses were going back to their houses. The sky was clear and the stars were twinkling like earthen lamps. Dashratha was sitting on a white marble seat. He felt as if something was lacking in him. He felt troubled. He was in such a state of mind that he felt like tearing his tight clothes. Then his attention went to his head's heaviness. He removed his crown and pushed it gently aside.

'What ails you, Dashratha?' asked his inner voice. Dashratha had some peace of mind. The inner voice he was waiting for had at last come to its consciousness. 'I- I feel troubled. I feel as if I were under the weight of the Himalayas.'

'Find out its reason!' guided his inner voice.

'Tried to discover! But I understood nothing.'

Dashratha took his brow in his hands.

'Dashratha, you know the reason! But you are hesitant in accepting it before me or that you're feeling shy. Just think, the longer you hide it from me, the more trouble you'll be in,' laughed the inner voice. 'Do you really get pleasure out of keeping yourself in woe and sorrow, Dashratha?'

'I say,' Dashratha gave in. He knew that if he remained silent much longer, the voice will rob him of his clothes.

'Speak out your trouble, your sorrow, your grief that is tormenting you so much. Speak out all that you've on your mind,' Dashratha's inner voice reassured him.

'The malady with me is that I've grown old. I don't understand why I'm still bearing the burden of being a king,' Dashratha cried as if with pain.

'To be a king is a burden for you, not your pleasure, O King!' The inner voice, it seemed, scolded Dashratha, 'Is upbringing of children a burden for a father? As a matter of fact the weal of a father lies hidden in the struggle undertaken by him to remove all the sorrows of his children.'

'Oh!' Dashratha beat his brow, 'I happened to use a wrong word. I wanted to say why I didn't pay my attention to this responsibility of mine to appoint Ayodhya's would-be crown prince and king.'

'This is your own problem, Dashratha! You've to take decision upon it.'

'All the ministers are in favour of Rama who is regarded as father or guardian by the people of Ayodhya. It is because it's he who takes care of them and so they shower their respect upon him. If it's so, why should I not liberate myself from my own responsibility of handing them over their father?' It seemed that Dashratha paid no attention to the comments of his own voice. He continued in his own way, 'It's the first time when I have come to know about Rama's competency and his popularity. Seeing

Rama's politeness and humility, I've always thought of him as an immature person.'

'It often happens so. Humility is taken to be a sign of cowardice and non-chivalry,' said the inner voice.

'Will you keep quiet for some time?' said Dashratha, feeling vexed. 'Whatever is striking my old mind, will be forgotten because of your preachings.'

The inner voice said nothing.

'What was I saying?' spoke Dashratha, feeling irritated.

'You were saying that you thought Rama to be an immature person because of his politeness,' said the voice.

Dashratha, as if staring at the voice, said, 'Is your duty only to whip me or shoot your arrows of taunts at me?'

' When Vishwamitra desired to take Rama with him to fight against demons, I had thought that he was still a child. At that time, I had indulged in making a hue and cry. But Vishwamitra flared up instead of being melted by my pleadings. I had to send Rama against my wishes for keeping up my reputation, and Rama insisted on taking Lakshmana with him...'

'If you hadn't sent Rama, what could Vishwamitra have done?'

'He could have damaged my reputation. Going from place to place, he could have announced that Raghukula's oath viz. 'Let life go, but not words' was a mere deception. Such a kind of statement uttered by Vishwamitra could have spread among the people of the entire kshatriya community and rishis like fire. It would have been a curse for me and I wouldn't have been able to show my face to anyone.'

'All is well that ends well', said the inner voice at a low pitch.

'Then Parashurama- a great enemy of kshatriyas!' Dashratha, as if he disregarded that voice, said, 'When I saw him, I was horrified. I felt that nobody could save my son, Rama from Parashurama, the enemy of kshatriyas. But Rama was able to tackle that situation by means of his self-confidence, courage and witticism. Since then I somewhat realised that of all the sons born out of yajna, Rama was the mightiest- a special being. I hadn't witnessed the incident of Shiva-bow being destroyed. Therefore, I had assumed that event would have been a matter of chance. But when Rama managed to launch Parashurama's Vaishnavi bow, I felt that Vishwamitra had truly made Rama more powerful than before. After the departure of Rama, I had expressed my sorrow before guru Vasishtha asking him why he hadn't intervened then, why he hadn't told Vishwamitra that Rama was still a child and so he couldn't have been pushed into trouble. Then guru Vasishtha had told me, "O King! How long will kshatriya prince Rama remain a child? Rama and his other brothers have received only bookish knowledge. They have no practical experience of real war or campaign. Someday or the other, such a situation will arise in the life of a kshatriya. If it is so, why not now? It's Rama's good luck that Vishwamitra himself has come to give Rama the practical knowledge of war- the person for whose blessings the entire world yearns. It's better to be killed while safeguarding the rishis with Vishwamitra than to die in an unknown war campaign like an inexperienced kshatriya. If for some reason or the other Rama encounters an honourable death, it will immortalize his name and Raghu dynasty's name. So, you can't run away from this situation, O King!"'

'Then I had realised that nobody could avert what was bound to happen. Many important departments of Ayodhya's administration have automatically gone into Rama's hands. Beautiful results are coming from all corners. At that time also I had thought it was because of my influence. But when today the head Acharya admired Rama and the public was full of joy and emotions after hearing the acharya and when the ministers and priests felt proud of him, I saw King Rama in the prince Rama.'

Saying so, Dashratha effortlessly rose from his seat and occupied lifelessly the bed-like swing in the northern part of the roof. The swing moved a little. Dashratha called the maid-servant and ordered her to push the swing gently. He told her that she could go if he dozed off. Today he would sleep under the cover of the open sky.

Dashratha's eyes began to sport with twinkling stars and his ears were attuned to the head Acharya's eulogy,

"It's my special request to kshatriya princes who have come here to receive education that they should study Rama's character. I've scripted Rama's noble character in different contexts. Their copies will soon be sent to the library as soon as they are ready. They can study them there, but Rama at present is in our midst. Whatever I've written about him, you should read and seek it in Rama's conduct. After this, you should assess and decide how much truth lies in what I've written about him. I'm extracting a part from that, and presenting before you some of Rama's qualities. I hope you'll enjoy yourself after hearing them. The first and foremost proof is that Rama is very handsome, charming and valiant." The head Acharya turned towards Rama and spoke with a smile on his face, "You can all see Rama's matchless handsomeness."

As he said so, the whole atmosphere was charged with joy. He continued, "He is placid and sweet-tongued. He gives no room to anyone's vices in his heart. If anyone obliges him even a little, he never forgets it. Whosoever comes to him, whether junior or senior, to him in rank, he converses with him with due respect and same tone."

These deep words of the head Acharya had led Dashratha's mind into thinking that he was now paying attention to them after being pointed out by the acharya. He noticed that whenever Rama talked with servants, he found the same sweetness and humility in his voice as when he talked with senior persons. But others don't do so. When he himself talks with any servant, there is a command in his voice. While talking with others he keeps in mind their position and moulds his voice accordingly.

"Rama is a lover of truth. There is no difference between his saying and doing. He is kind-hearted, ethical and conqueror of his senses. He is most pious and noble. He shelters those who seek his shelter. He is apathetic towards vicious deeds. He makes no contribution to them. On the contrary, he presents his logic against them and like Guru Jupiter (Brahaspati) in favour of justice. The very essence of all ages is known to Rama. It appears as if Destiny, the creator had put all the essence of the grandest men and sages in Rama. You may take this statement of mine somewhat exaggerated. I've no problem. But whatever I've seen or felt, I've submitted before you as it is so that it may magnify your joy."

This last statement of the head Acharya, it seemed, had made the people mad out of joy. They were beyond pacification. Then the head Acharya requested guru Vashishtha to express his views about Rama. It seemed as if the crowd of people had held their breath to hear what guru Vasishtha would say. Vashishtha kept standing silently for a moment. It appeared as if he was finding it difficult to get the beginning of his expression or he had lost in his own thoughts. He said, "I'm Vasishtha, Rama's guru, who has judged Rama from closet quarters. That Vasishtha vindicates each and every word of the head Acharya about

Rama to be true- very true. There is no flattery of any kind in it. Nor is there any motto to please the sovereign. It is the head Acharya's beautiful and devotional speech." On hearing Vasishtha's statement, the entire people began to jump and scream out of joy. Vasishtha turned towards the head Acharya. The head Acharya folded his hands in devotion to great guru Vashishtha. Vashishtha with a smile on his face raised his right hand to bless him. Vashishtha said, "I would like to tell the head teacher about Rama's certain special qualities which are not known to others or which can't be seen in normal conditions." He paused for a while and then said, "Rama understands the true essence of renouncing things and stocking them. Outwardly, you'll feel that Rama hasn't done a right thing by abandoning this thing or by doing that thing. But religiosity resides in his soul. He knows what religion is, which is a very small incident. Hence ordinary eyes are not appropriate to judge Rama's conduct. One needs divine eyes to understand his character and deeds. I'm saying this, not without any solid proof. When Brahamarishi Vishwamitraji demanded Rama to fight against demons' terror and if there had been any other kshtriya prince in his place, he could have said that he would not accompany Vishwamitra, leaving behind his luxurious, protected and convenient life.

It was that Vishwamitra who wished to take Rama to the Region of Death. After Rama's departure, many kshtriyas spoke ill of Rama's deed as something suicidal.

They said that it was far away from Rama's far-sightedness. They said that though the Maharaja and his counsellors had termed this deed right and just yet none could have done anything if Rama hadn't agreed to go. But Rama's intellect and devotion... All eminent and lofty people. Howsoever majestic the Himalayas would be, its reflection would appear to be smaller in the mirror. Therefore, from ordinary perspective, Rama's grand character would appear to be small. So, I say one needs a divine vision to see and feel him."

Vashishtha held his breath for a while and cast his fleeting looks upon the people. He said, "Rama suffers neither from anger, nor malice nor false pride, the greatest enemy of man. Rama is the controller of illusions. If there is anything in Rama, it is spirituality and renunciation. He is in possession of a simple, natural and the most beautiful feeling of performing one's duty."

Repeating Rama's virtues, Dashratha's entire personality was aglow with joy. He was astonished to note what was happening to him from inside. When these orators were speaking, he kept sitting indolently, simply nodding his head a little. But now when he was sitting in isolation, thinking of Rama's admiration, every pore of his body was filled with a wave of joy. Dashratha felt a quake of greatest intensity within himself and tears gushed out of his eyes. He was awake. Midnight had passed. The maid-servant had gone, taking him to be asleep. Dashratha stood in the balcony. He felt as if people standing on the premises down or in rooftops of buildings were trying to have a look of him. There was zeal and excitement among people. 'Look at Maharaja Dashratha, father of God like King Rama. We feel gratified after catching a sight of such a grand father whose son is unparalleled.' Dashratha could hear clearly how he was being showered with indescribable honour for being Rama's father.

'I don't understand why I'm still occupying the position of a king,' Dashratha felt embarrassed. He said as if he were speaking to himself, 'It often occurs that immediately after the king's death, the crown prince is made the king in the midst of grief and sorrow. His coronation takes place only in name. The people find themselves in a fix whether they should have condolence meeting at the death of the previous king or celebrate the occasion of the new king's ascendency to the throne.'

'The intoxication of position doesn't let a person do all this, O King!' the inner voice arose. It continued, 'The happiness arising from power, its tempting essence makes him feel that he is the best of all. There are many kings who can neither see nor hear clearly. They are afflicted with physical ailment and spend most of their time in their beds lying like corpses. Somehow or the other, they make efforts to attend the royal meetings and sometimes they are brought to their throne. But they are always afflicted with the lust of being called a king. Even their sons long for their death so that they may be crowned as kings. But social courtesy and social norms don't allow them to push their father from the royal seat. Even their ministers mock at their plight. They still remain glued to their seat like the blind and the deaf.'

'But my Rama is not one of them,' spoke Dashratha at once.

'How should I construe your sentence?' the voice smiled. It continued, 'What does it mean that Rama is not so? Does it mean that you want to remain stuck to your seat even in your old age?'

Dashratha has always found himself besieged by this voice. Whenever it rises in him, it torments him and denounces him; it tortures him and insults him. If need arises, it renders him naked standing before the mirror. It doesn't take into consideration that he is the king. It rather becomes more violent and more severe on knowing that he is the king.

'No, it doesn't mean that,' Dashratha looked at it with severity and anger. 'It means I'm going to coronate Rama in the near future.'

'In the future...' There was sarcasm in the voice. It seemed that it will lose its life laughingly on hearing this taunt. 'In future...Ahaa Dashratha! It means that when you are breathing your last, and lying in an unconscious condition you'll call out Rama and say - I hand over the charge of Ayodhya kingdom to you. And after this last sentence, the queens will be weeping bitterly.'

'Will you ever listen to me calmly?'Dashratha wanted that once, only once his voice should embody itself and come before him, and then he would make it silent forever.

'O.K. Say, Maharaja Dashratha,' the voice was not able to control its laughter.

Dashratha said bitterly, 'Coronation is not like a daily bath to be given to the crown prince and then make him sit on the royal throne. Its preparation and its norms take their own time.'

'That time elapsed long, long ago, Dashratha!' snubbed his voice. 'Now you're awake and so don't sleep over the matter. Why don't you perform it next morning itself?'

'Tomorrow!'

'Yes, tomorrow.'

'It's not possible,' Dashratha laughed at the voice's childish credo.

'But it's not impossible also,' said the voice. 'You know within your heart of hearts that you can do it. O King! Try to understand its joy and greatness. Up till now no other king has ever done so. You will be called unique, wise, ethical and lover of the people. You'll enjoy it as much as you enjoyed your sons' weddings. Present a living example of yours before the entire society of royal kshtriyas. They should look upon you as their ideal. They should follow in your foot-steps. Now leaving aside negative thoughts, do something as early as possible so that Rama may have his coronation under the pious, happy stars.

Dashratha rang the bell to summon the guard. At once many guards arrived. As a matter of fact, the bell rang unintentionally two or three times. Dashratha came to realise this when he saw a large number of soldiers. Seeing Dashratha in anxiety standing in the balcony, the body guards became active and began to search for the enemy here and there.

"Victory to the Maharaja!" The chief body-guard bowed his head. He asked, "What happened, Maharaja?'

"Nothing. By mistake the emergency bell rang", said Dashratha, trying to sit on his seat.

The chief guard sent all the other soldiers back. He stood before Dashratha and asked, "Maharaja! If you're feeling unwell, shall I call in the royal physician?"

Dashratha looked at the Chief guard and then bent his head while sitting. The chief guard kept standing in wait for his reply.

"Send immediately my special messenger to all the Chief councilors with the message that they should all attend the most urgent meeting on time immediately after the completion of the morning yajna."

* * *

12

Dashratha cast his fleeting looks upon his councillors. All were present in their own respective places. It was clear from their facial expression that they were eager to know why an emergency meeting had been summoned all of a sudden.

Dashratha greeted guru Vasishtha with a view to seeking his permission. Vasishtha also gave his consent by way of gesture.

"All the present Gentlemen!" There was a mix of pride, affection and seriousness. "It's known to all that my ancestors have always looked after the people of Ayodhya like their children. I've always walked upon their guided paths of truth and renown and I have always worked for the welfare of the people to my utmost capability and knowledge. I've grown old physically while serving the people. Now I have begun to feel that I'm no longer in a position to continue to bear the burden of state administration. There was a time when it afforded me a great pleasure, but now it has become a burden for me. I want to take respite from it. My ardent desire is to appoint my son, Shri Rama, to look after the subject with the consent of the wise people. Shri Rama

is much better than I am so as far as virtues are concerned. He is as valiant as Lord Indra in conquering the enemies. The fact is that you people know more about Shri Rama than I do. I know him only as much as I have heard about him from you. There is much which is left to be known; I hope I'll come to know that also through you. Tomorrow morning, I'll appoint Shri Rama as the crown prince of Ayodhya under the happy stars. Soon after his coronation and shifting the burden of the kingdom on to his shoulders, I want to be free from all anxieties forever. I expect you to advise me how it will possibly be arranged. Besides this, if you're thinking of something else for the welfare of the public, you may apprise me of it without any hesitation."

Dashratha noticed that on hearing this, all the present councilors had a wave of joy. They began to discuss it among themselves. Dashratha looked at them pleasantly and in a contented voice said, "I shall be pleased if you express your feelings before me."

There was complete silence in the meeting.

Sumantra rose from his seat. He looked towards all the councilors to know whether there was anybody else to wish to say something. When he felt assured that nobody else had anything to say and that they were waiting to hear him, he said, "This decision of the Maharaja is unique and joyful. We all agree to it. According to the wishes of the Maharaja, a special messenger will be sent to all friendly kings to invite them to come to Ayodhya tomorrow. But the kings of Mithila and Kekaya will take more than a week to reach here."

"We were astonished when Mithila's king, Janaka had invited us to Rama's wedding. We will also astonish them with the auspicious news of Rama's coronation", laughed Dashratha. "So far as Kekaya's king is concerned, he will not take it ill if in his absence this significant celebration takes place."

"We agree with you, Maharaja! But we wish you to express your innermost feelings. What happened that obliges you to see Shri Rama to be coronated as the crown prince tomorrow morning itself?" Sumantra expressed his curiosity to know this. He continued, "Maharaja! I'm asking you only because there is every possibility of many questions being raised by the public and other members of Kshtriya society why Rama's coronation is being performed in emergency."

"I agree with you", said Dashratha in his serious voice. But my heart is full of infinite vexation and its only remedy is Rama's coronation. You simply tell me if there is any obstacle of any kind in this noble venture."

"Maharaja! We can't express how happy we are at your far-sighted decision. We ourselves want to see Rama mounted on giant elephant under the white umbrella passing through Ayodhya. This pageantry will be worth-seeing."

"Very beautiful!" Dashratha was over-joyed. His eyes were bright with happiness. He said, "Councillors! An idea has sprung up in my mind all of a sudden. I hope you won't interpret it in any other sense. I'm simply asking you", paused Dashratha and gazed at everybody. He said, "I have been looking after my subject most religiously. I don't think there is any affliction being suffered from by anybody. So, when I put forward the proposal of Rama's coronation before you, you all agreed to it without delay. Why didn't anyone of you tell me that it was not so, that I had not grown old. What's the need of Shri Rama's coronation as long as I'm alive? Why do you want to see Shri Rama as the king even though I'm alive?"

All the councilors looked at Dashratha in surprise. Quite often does Dashratha seek advice of his advisers from different angles. He never wants that the members of the council should ever agree to his unjust decision either out of fear or greed. "It's because Shri Rama is better than you in respect of virtues", said one councillor. "Now Maharaja, don't ask us to throw light on your vices."

The council burst into laughter. Dashratha also joined them in laughter.

"This statement had been made by the Maharaja himself in the beginning of his talk." That assembly said, "We look upon Shri Rama as the young Dashratha or his now edition. We see no difference between you and Shri Rama. Shri Rama is your expansion, Maharaja! So, we all want that God should emerge in His giant form instead of pigmy form like Vaman incarnation."

Again, there was a ripple of laughter. This reply given to Dashratha was as if Dashratha had taken his bath in the river Ganges.

"Friend!" Dashratha called Sumantra affectionately.

"Yes, Maharaja!"

"Fetch Rama here at once."

Sumantra bowed his head and set out.

"Please take your breakfast until Sumantra accompanied by Shri Rama returns." At the gesture of Dashratha, breakfast was served to all councillors.

"Bhagwana!" Dashratha spoke to Guru Vasishtha, "Whatever is needed for Shri Rama's coronation, kindly order the servants to make preparation for it."

Vasishtha said to the servants, "As soon as the sun rises tomorrow, mantras will be chanted for peace and the well-being of the world. Invite the Brahmins and arrange for their seats. Arrange for sending to the yajna chamber all the articles like gold, gems, herbs, white garlands, honey, pure ghee, new clothes, flags, white sceptre- a sign of royal honour, gold vases, two fans made from the hair growing on the cow's tail, a bull whose horn is covered with gold and many other needed things. The palace, inner apartments and all the city doors must be adorned with strings of sandalwood and fragrant incenses. Flags must be unfurled all around the city. Fragrant water must be sprinkled on highways. The balconies of palaces should be occupied by musicians and dancers. The security of the entire Ayodhya should be handed over to the army. The special bodyguards should be appointed for the palace's premises." After giving instructions to the authorities concerned, Vasishtha bade good-bye.

While sitting in the midst of councilors, Dashratha saw Rama coming along with Sumantra. When the king saw Rama's carefree and superb gait, his face's brilliance and magnanimity, he felt as if he were seeing Rama for the first time. He was feeling fascinated by him.

Climbing up the steps with Sumantra, Rama came close to the throne. He folded his hands to greet Dashratha and bowed his head. Dashratha rose up suddenly. Pulling Rama's hand, he embraced Rama. With tears welled up in his eyes, he said smilingly, "Rama!" and with a gesture of his hand, he told Rama to sit on the gold throne built specially for his coronation. Then he told Rama aloud so that all the councilors could hear him, "Son! You are born to my eldest queen Kaushalya. There is no doubt that you are more virtuous than I am. It's a matter of pride for any country that the king's son is imbued with more qualities than the King himself. It's, therefore, my desire that tomorrow morning you accept to be the crown prince under the pious and happy stars. Son! I expect you to keep in your mind the royal power and set up before the public the example of an ideal prince by your good conduct. One has to look after the people by means of his ethics and justice. Though there was no need for me to say anything of this sort to a virtuous son like you yet I have said this laconically as a matter of formality and with a sense of my responsibility."

As soon as Dashratha became silent, all the councilors began to congratulate Rama loudly. Rama kept accepting their good wishes with courtesy and bowed head like a statue. The council was adjourned. Rama greeted Dasharatha and guru Vasishtha, and sought their permission to go back to his palace.

× × ×

Rama's chariot stopped on the premises of the grand building. He alighted and strode towards the steps which he climbed. Gate-keepers and servants were greeting him with great enthusiasm. Nobody congratulated him but their happy faces were telling him that they had knowledge of some good news.

"Seetey!" Rama called out.

"Arya!" the maid-servant bowed her head and said, "The mistress has gone to Mother Kaushalya's palace." Rama thought, 'It's good. I'll convey this happy news to mother and she'll feel very happy.'

Rama washed his face and hands, drank a little water and then proceeded to Mother Kaushalya's palace. Hardly had he stepped down when he saw Sumantra's chariot coming towards him with great speed.

"SumantraJi!" Rama said to himself, 'to come behind me so speedily now! I hope everything is well. Sumantra is not an ordinary servant who will be sent for some ordinary matter. He is the king's special minister, true friend and the chief councilor.'

Getting down from the chariot, Rama advanced forward and held Sumantra by his hand. He asked, "All of a sudden, you are in such speed..." "Crown Prince! Maharaja has called you." The very voice of Sumantra was telling him that Dashratha was in great trouble.

"Speak clearly. What's the matter?" Rama wanted to know its reason.

"You have been summoned at once. Now it's your decision whether you want to go or not."

Rama looked at Sumantra who had never talked to him like this before. What's its secret?

He boarded Sumantra's chariot.

"Charioteer! Carry me to the Maharaja", ordered Rama.

The chariot caught speed.

"Crown Prince! You didn't take your own chariot."

"SumantraJi! I thought of having heart- to- heart talk with you."

"Say!"

"At present I am neither in the royal assembly nor have I been coronated. Then why are you addressing me by way of formality? It distances me from you." There was a touch of love in Rama's voice. He said, "We have sought our growth under your guidance as sons do. I hope and request you to address me in an informal way." Rama paused, and to know his reaction he looked towards Sumantra. Sumantra smiled and patted Rama's hand affectionately. Rama said, "Maharaja's state is not hidden from you. What happened in the present that obliged the Maharaja to send you to summon me in emergency?"

"Rama, after your departure, the Maharaja inspected all the arrangements connected with tomorrow's celebration and then went into his chamber. After some time he called me. I saw the Maharaja pacing up and down in great tension. As he saw me, he said, "Friend! You fetch Rama at once. I find myself and Rama unsafe on account of doubts, suspicions and ill-omens. I have to hold secret talks with Rama on some very important issue."

"Maharaja is very sensitive." Sumantra said, "Any ill thought or ill sign perplexes him. No doubt, he is brave but at the same time he is tender-hearted. He rejoices soon and gets perplexed also."

"SumantraJi! Tell the royal physician to prescribe some medicine for the Maharaja so that all his sinews become strong and healthy. The rest he may do whatever he deems fit", said Rama.

"I also feel that the reason behind it is his physical debility", said Sumantra as if he were in chime with Rama.

× × ×

As Rama entered the palace, he saw Dashratha pacing up and down in tension as Sumantra had told him. It seemed that he didn't take rest after sending Sumantra. Dashratha was so much absorbed in his own gloomy thoughts that he didn't notice Rama standing before him .As they exchanged looks, Rama bent to touch his feet. As before,Dashratha stopped Rama from doing so and clung Rama to his chest. He said, "Rama, whenever you come to see me, you ought to fall in my arms. As I embrace you, I feel most vigorous and most energetic."

"Your advice is of supreme importance to me, father! But if I do so, it will be an act of discourtesy on my part. If all my brothers and people including the youth see me doing so, they will forget the culture of bowing. Father! Let me discharge my own ethical duties. Our growth and joy lie hidden in it", Rama folded his hands to greet him.

"There is nobody else like you in this world, Rama!" spoke Dashratha in pride. Rama paid no attention to what Dashratha said. He thought that it was a father's sentiment for him. Just as every mother looks upon her child as the most handsome and matchless one, in the same way, Maharaja Dashratha is also looking upon me from a father's perspective. This is nothing but a natural human quality.

"Father, tell me what I should do for you so that you may feel contented and happy", Rama wanted to know why he was called.

"Sit by me, son", Dashratha sat on his bed and asked Rama by the gesture of his hand to sit beside him. Then he stood up and said, "Let us go inside, Rama!" Without knowing Rama's reaction, he moved towards the inner chamber.

Rama followed him but began to think, 'What has happened to father? Ayodhya is so much safe and secure that the Maharaja can talk with him at any public place, path or crossing.'

"Look Rama!" Dashratha held Rama by his hand and made him sit beside himself. Then he said, "Whatever duties I had as a king, as a father or a son or a pupil, I have discharged them with full integrity and honesty. According to the scriptures, whatever debts, a man has to bear, I have freed myself from all of them. My only duty in this old age is to lie at the feet of Shri Narayana after handing over this kingdom to you. Hence, whatever orders I give to you, you should obey them."

"Father! Every wish of yours for me is like the utterances of Brahma. Orders are given only when there is some doubt about the fulfillment of wishes." There was a tinge of love for father in Rama's voice. He said, "But I feel that you find yourself insecure. Please tell me its reason."

"Rama!" Dashratha's voice was shaky. His body was also quivering a little. He said, "These days I am dreaming of many inauspicious and horrible things. It seems as if meteors were exploding in the sky during the daytime and were falling upon me. Astrologers say that Sun, Mars and Rahu have made their most terrible assault upon my birth zodiac. If a king is besieged by such ill omens, he becomes the victim of the greatest malady and at last loses his life."

"Are you afraid of death?" Rama asked, feeling somewhat astonished.

Dashratha had never expected such a kind of question. He went on looking at Rama and said, "Rama! A kshatriya is not scared of death."

"But father, that often happens so in the battle-field. At that time he is full of excitement and zeal and then he becomes fearless." Rama's voice was simple. He said, "To be afraid of death is a natural phenomenon of every human-being. But I know that you are not scared of death. You are worried about Ayodhya."

"Yes, Rama!" Dashratha took in deep breath. He was happy that Rama was trying to penetrate the secret reason of his fear. He said, "Rama! Your coronation mustn't be postponed in any circumstance. Whatever be, you must get yourself coronated as soon as the moon enters the holy planet tomorrow because man's mind is infirm. I don't want that the black clouds of lust overcast my heart and result in an unhappy happening."

"Perhaps you want to say that your decision may change. Even then there is nothing to worry about. You are the king. You are at full liberty to change your decision, and you've every right to do so", Rama gave his plea to Dashratha to remove his doubts.

"No, Rama! You are not trying to understand me. As a matter of fact, you can't understand", said Dashratha as if he felt vexed. "You simply listen to me and then try to understand me."

"If you are ill at ease when I put a question to you in an effort to understand you, it's O.K. I'll not put any question to you."

"No, Rama! It's not so." Dashratha felt that he was getting more perplexed than what was necessary for him. He tried to make him look normal and then said, "There is every likelihood of an obstacle rising in auspicious things. You should, therefore, keep fast with good feelings from this time onward till next morning. You should have your coronation over until Bharata returns from his maternal uncle's house."

"Bharata!" Rama looked at Dashratha without batting his eye lashes and with mouth wide open in surprise. When Sumantra came behind him to take him to the king, he had thought what had happened that obliged Maharaja to send Sumantra immediately because till then the king was feeling rejoiced. Truly, the Maharaja's mental condition is very deplorable. He is talking of unnecessary things. It looks that there is no coordination between his tongue and his mind. The Maharaja seems to be losing his thinking power on account of too much acidity or any other physical ailment. Rama said as if warning Dashratha, "Father, you have just told me that I should remain in safe custody of my own men along with Sita. On the contrary, you're telling me that my coronation should be over before Bharata returns. Bharata is my brother, my cordial younger brother. I have affiliation with him. But your statement tells me that he is my enemy. If you want to know from me, I'm feeling bad that Bharata will not be present on this auspicious occasion. But I have no other means but to obey your orders."

"There is no doubt about it, Rama! Bharata respects you, loves you. He is your devotee. He is ethical, kind and has control over his passions. But many times it so happens that even great souls become the victims of ill-will, jealousy and envy because of the impact of many reasons." Dashratha said philosophically.

"Then you should have taken into consideration Lakshmana's presence and Shatrughana's absence. Why did you accuse only Bharata of this? Not 'accuse' but a stigma on Bharata?" Rama ensnared Dashratha.

"Oh, Rama!" Finding himself in Rama's snare, Dashratha beat his brow and began to think, "Rama is so much adept in logic that it is impossible to outbeat him. It is truly said about Rama that he is as good in logic as Guru Jupiter so far as ethics and justice are concerned. If I try to entrap Rama in unnecessary things, I will myself be in Rama's trap. He said, "Rama! When a man is not at peace with himself, he begins to talk in an odd manner. Then he begins to talk about his bad dreams seen in his unconscious sleeping state. Rama! Whatever I have said about coronation and fast, you should follow them. Now Rama! You can go, Sumantra is awaiting you."

Rama greeted Dashratha. Rama's eyes were saying, 'Father! You're hiding something from me. That's why you are ordering me to go from here so that I may not read your innermost feelings.' Dashratha's eyes read the message of Rama's eyes and they hung in shame. Rama turned to go. Sumantra was waiting for him in an outer apartment.

The chariot moved. During this time Sumantra didn't ask Rama what transpired between him and Dashratha. Nor did he ask him about Dashratha's mental state or about the gravity of the situation. Rama broke in, "Sumantraji! Why is the Maharaja looking upon Bharata as my enemy? Can you tell me something about it?"

Sumantra listened to Rama and kept quiet. While thinking, he was making his ring swing round.

"If you want to keep it secret from me, I will not insist you to tell me about it because it is not proper to leak out the secret without the king's permission."

"Rama!" said Sumantra in a low voice, "I've not yet arrived at any conclusion about it. There are many things which are compelling me to think more about it. I'm myself analyzing the whole situation. Existing conditions have undergone a sudden change. Something has transported the Maharaja from joy to sorrow and from doubt to worry. Keeping your passions under control, you should do what the Maharaja has asked you to do. Spend the night with caution and care."

Rama looked towards Sumantra. He thought how Sumantra knew about controlling the passions and spending the night under tight security. Does it mean that the Maharaja has already discussed this matter with Sumantra? Maybe, he wanted Sumantra to tell me all this and then he changed his mind and thought it better to convey it to me himself. Rama was eyeing Sumantra off and on. His silence was telling Rama that Sumantraji did know something secret about it but he wanted to keep it secret.

× × ×

Soon after Rama's departure, Dashratha heaved a sigh of relief. His condition was that of a criminal who was being glared at by an official and luckily he had spared him thinking that he was innocent.

He sipped some water and let himself fall on his bed. He was running a severe headache. He fisted his forehead and felt as if his entire head was like stone He was repenting over what he said to Rama that the latter should have his coronation in the absence of Bharata from Ayodhya. Dashratha was frowning upon himself thinking that he couldn't keep control over himself. If Rama went straight to Kaikeyi and asked her out of curiosity why father was saying so about Bharata, he would be in hot soup. Thinking so, his throat went dry and he sipped many glasses of water. Again, Dashratha began to beat his brow with his fists, 'Why, why did the word 'Bharara' came out of his mouth? Couldn't I remain silent?'

'Dashratha! Fisting your forehead would be of no avail. You had.better strike your head against the wall, ' Dashratha's inner voice laughed. It said, 'You've been preaching Rama about the control of sense organs. What about your own sense organs?'

Dashratha ground his teeth. 'Whenever I find myself in such a state, my inner voice adds fuel to the fire.'

'Don't worry. Rama won't go to Kaikeyi,' laughed his inner voice.

'How do you know this? Are you Rama? Or has Rama told you so? Or Rama won't go to Kaikeyi without your permission. I'm astonished to see the relation between Rama and Kaikeyi. Rama looks upon Kaikeyi as if she were his real mother. He is inclined more to Kaikeyi than to Kaushalya and Sumitra. You will see that Rama along with Sita will first go to Kaikeyi to give this news to her and to seek her blessings.' Dashratha's voice was out of temper.

'It is but natural that a son with his wife will go to his mothers,' his voice raised an objection. 'If Rama went to Kaikeyi out of the way and happened to tell her how I took Bharata to be his enemy, I would feel undone.'

'Rama is faultless in this context. You yourself happened to leak out the secret of your heart. Now if Rama happened to share it with his mothers and brother Lakshmana, there would be no astonishment,' laughed the inner voice.

"Hey Rama!" Dashratha breathed this out. His face turned pale.

'But Rama will never do so,' said the inner voice placidly.

'How?' Dashratha saw the silver lining in the midst of clouds. 'Because you too have accepted and here all others acknowledge that Rama is wiser than Dashratha. I definitely believe that Rama might have disregarded it,' the voice expressed its opinion.

'Let it be so! Let your word be true!' Dashratha felt that if his inner voice had a body, he would have embraced it.

* * *

13

Sumantra parted from Rama at Kaushalya's inner chamber. Rama saw that every man-servant and maid-servant and all other officials looked very happy on seeing him. Rama felt that all his well-wishers had already conveyed the news of his coronation to Sita and his mother. Rama noticed that Mother Kaushalya in her silk dress was standing before Shri Narayana's idol and was offering her prayers. Sumitra, brother Lakshmana and Sita were standing behind Kaushalya with their folded hands in prayer.

Rama was astonished to note that Mother Kaikeyi wasn't present there. All of a sudden, he cursed himself for thinking so. 'Often does Kaikeyi remain in her inner chamber. Even on occasions of ordinary worships, it's only Sumitra who is seen with Kausalya. And today also it is the same.' thought Rama. He composed himself. He went to his mother who was completely absorbed in her silent thoughts and called out, "Mother!"

When Kaushalya saw Rama bowing his head, she patted him. It appeared from her eyes that she was full of gratitude towards Shri Narayana and she was proud of Rama as well.

"Congratulations, Son!"

'Oh! I was rightly guessing,' smiled Rama within himself.

"Long live my son! May Lakshmi bless you! Let all the enemies in your way be destroyed!" Kaushalya kissed Rama on his forehead. Rama thought,'Why has his Mother Kaushalya forgotten to mention Mother Kaikeyi? Why do the differences exist between them? Has the news of his coronation created ill-will in her? I know they are not on happy relations with each other. But I never thought that the matter would go so deep with them.'

"Son! You were born of me under some auspicious stars that you pleased your father by means of your virtues. At present, Maharaja Dashratha is thinking of nobody else except you. You have become the soul of his life."

Rama was trying to discover in his Mother Kaushalya's voice whether her words conveyed her natural happiness or haughtiness.

"Rama, I had fasted to achieve you from the Lotus-eyed Lord Vishnu. Today I have got success. The Lord has given you His own image."

Rama couldn't arrive at any conclusion. He kept on finding out the inner meaning of Kaushalya's words.

"Mother, father wants me and Sita to exercise restraint on ourselves and keep fast also tonight. You are, therefore, requested to make me and Sita do whatever you deem fit."

Rama found Lakshmana in a happy mood, gazing at him. He took him in his arms and said, "Lakshmana, you are my second inner self. This royal power is coming to you. You should take care of this earth with me. Always think of the welfare of the common people and do accordingly."

After taking permission from his mothers, Rama went to his palace.

× × ×

Dashratha implored Vasishtha to go to Rama to guide him about yajna, the fast and other rites to be performed tonight and tomorrow morning. After Vashishtha's departure, Dashratha was once again in solitude. He thought of summoning Sumantra so that he could have long talks with him and get tired to have sound sleep. But he knew that he was sleepless. He started walking up and down and here and there quite fast as he wanted to know the cause of his restlessness. Sometimes he drank water and sometimes he wiped the drops of perspiration from his forehead. Sometimes he sat on his cot and sometimes on a stool. But these activities increased his restlessness. At last, Dashratha felt disappointed and sat on the ground. When he found his sitting uncomfortable, he let himself lie down on the ground. His eyes were fixed on the ceiling. His breath and heart-rate was abnormal.

'On this auspicious occasion you should have been with your friends and relatives in a theatre, Dashratha. No doubt, nobody said anything about it to you. But you are expected to celebrate this occasion with them now. Be happy yourself and keep others happier.' Dashratha's inner voice spoke to him. It added, ' What will the invited kings and state representatives think suddenly about you on this occasion? What will happen to your courtesy and popularity? They may dub you a haughty king. They may say that since they are under the suzerainty of King Dashratha, they are bound to be present in the coronation of Rama. Since they are less mighty than him, Dashratha has taken an undue advantage of their weakness by disregarding them.'

'Dashratha has never disregarded anyone,' said Dashratha, feeling vexed.

'All right! Just repeat your statement a bit,' commented the inner voice.

'What is the need of repetition? One can be disregarded out of ignorance. You take no time in making a mountain out of molehill,' Dashratha felt infuriated.

'O King! Till yesterday you disregarded Rama and his mother Kaushalya. Today the same Rama has now become the breath of your life because you know that you stand nowhere without Rama. Now when you are going to coronate that Rama, why are you not happy?' said the voice. It became aggressive and said, 'If I say that you're unhappy because you have to relinquish your kingship, you will try to pounce upon me. You should, therefore, tell me the reason of your vexation. Don't tell me that you don't know. Every person knows why he is in woe. But he keeps on covering it with many reasons. He thinks that if he expresses the reason of his sorrow, the society will take him to be infirm, vicious and diseased.'

'Bharata is the cause of my worry,' said Dashratha.

'Why? asked the voice. It added,' So far as Lakshmana is concerned, he happens to look at Rama from the view-point of a friend. But Bharata's case is different. He is devoted to Rama like a servant, like a devotee. He worships him as if he were God. Shatrughana sees the image of father in Rama. And you are casting aspersions on Bharata, saying that he is an obstacle in the way of Rama. Do you think that breath can ever be an enemy of one's life? It is the life spring of body.'

'If that breath checks itself from its process, then?' reasoned Dashratha.

'Dashratha, what has happened to you?'asked the voice. You have forgotten the simple principle of physiology. Breath can never withhold itself from its function. It is nature's mystery that breath remains active even when all the sense organs become loose and even the mind becomes inactive.'

'I am not afraid of Bharata but of his grandpa's,' Dashratha changed the direction of his topic.

'Okay, now you should throw some light on the scare you are likely to get from his grandpa's,' It seemed as if the voice was ready to disapprove every thought of Dashratha.

'Even today do I remember that the Keykaya king had a crushing defeat at my hands in the war. He had begun to think I would make him a prisoner of war or kill him. But he was extremely happy when there was a proposal of alliance from my side. Then somebody had advised him that if he gave his daughter Kaikeyi to me in marriage, there would be family relations, and not that of a subordinate king. Such a sort of politics is an ordinary thing in Kshatriya society. Kaikeyi plucked the chord of my heart. Immediately I sent a letter of invitation to Keykaya king for nupital relations. No doubt, Kaikeyi was too young for me. Yet she agreed to marry me, sacrificing all her wishes in order to safeguard the kingdom and its people.' At that time Keykaya king had said to me amusingly, "Maharaja Dashratha! My ardent desire is that a son born to Kaikeyi should be Ayodhya's king. Do you agree to it?" Dashratha became silent for a while and then spoke, "I accept this."

'It was only a joke. It often happens so. There is no need of giving too much importance to it.' The voice tried to make him understand. It seemed as if it took pity on Dashratha this time.

'No, it was not a joke. I was serious then.' Dashratha grew excited.

'Were you serious or stupid?' The voice took Dashratha to task. 'I'm trying to make you understand that it was a simple joke which people generally indulge in on wedding occasions, and you are getting panicky knowingly. Many times you have told your friends, etc. that this kingdom, this palace, this army belongs to you. But has it happened so?'

'But this is a different matter.'

'How is it different? Tell me'.

'Bharata's maternal uncle Yudhajita from the side of Keykaya king will strongly protest against it.'

'Did he object to it?'

'He has no information about Rama's coronation to be held tomorrow. Nor has he got any invitation card!' Dashratha put forward his argument, 'Don't I understand why Yudhajita has kept on visiting Ayodhya continually and kept Bharata with him for a long time? He is instructing Bharata that he himself is the king of Ayodhya declared by Dashratha. He will, therefore, have to fight for his rights.'

'Aha! Maharaja!' It seemed as if the inner voice made fun of Dashratha for his childish argument by clapping. 'Maharaja! Tell me one thing. Did Yudhajita or Keykaya's king ever remind you of your promise? Did either of them ever say that he was awaiting the time when you would hand over Ayodhya's rein to Bharata?'

'No, they never expressed their view or feeling about it,' said Dashratha.

'Then why are you torturing yourself by charging them with your ill- feelings?'

'They are waiting for the chance.'

'O.K.!' The voice was astonished. 'Kaikeyi is still here. Did she ever say so?'

'Never.'

'Now when she is familiar with this news, has she protested against this?'

'No.'

'Then, Dashratha! Compose yourself. Don't trouble yourself for what has not occurred,' the inner voice tried to make him understand. 'Many times man's will power begins to think so ill that it seems that that incident wouldn't have occurred if it hadn't been thought so. It's not true to say that if you think ill of someone, he will suffer in his life. So, Dashratha! Be at peace with yourself. Only peace, peace, peace.'

Dashratha felt sleepy now.

× × ×

With resolution for yajna, Rama and Sita were on the mat made of wild grass on the ground. After offering evening prayer to Shri Narayana, they were discussing with quiet mind.

"The entire episode occurred so fast that I couldn't get time to go to Mother Kaikeyi because of the coming and going of someone or the other, necessary information, father's orders and advice of gurus."

"After coronation you may go to Mother Kaikeyi, Aryaputra! Her joy will know no bounds when she sees you in that dress," said Sita. She added, "My most beloved husband! I've heard only in stories about such reciprocal love and warm feelings. When you are sitting with Mother Kaikeyi, Lakshmana with Mother Kausalya and Bharata, Shatrughana with Mother Sumitra and Kaikeyi, it becomes impossible to know who is whose mother. There is wonderful love of all sons towards all mothers and vice-versa."

"Yes, Seetey!" said Rama. "It is all due to Shri Narayana's grace that Raghu clan knows the essence of love and has made it the soul of its life. When Mother Kaikeyi gazes at me, she gets absorbed in a wholly. It is like the mother who feels gratified when she gazes at her new-born child."

There was a well-armed batallion of bodyguards outside Rama's chamber. The Chief bodyguard sought Rama's permission to enter.

"Speak out, Chief bodyguard!"

"Prince! Maharaja has given strict orders that we must all be very cautious and careful till tomorrow morning. There must not be any indolence or carelessness on our part." The chief bodyguard paused.

"Put aside your hesitation, Chief!" Smiled Rama.

"There is another order also that only the close relatives should be allowed to meet you, and nobody else. But the Sage Narada has just arrived and he wants to see you."

"Chief bodyguard!" said Rama with warm feeling, placing his hand on his shoulder. "It is well-known about the Sage Narada that he doesn't visit any place but appears. He is affiliated with the entire world."

"I know his value, Prince!"

"I hope you haven't read out the Maharaja's orders to him?"

"Prince!" the Chief bodyguard bowed his head and added, "In the Maharaja's kingdom sages, ascetics and brahmins are adored. Who can dare utter such words before them?"

"Then let's move. Let me offer my greetings at the feet of the sage."

As Rama got into the chamber, he saw Narada in an ecstatic mood. Narada was playing his one-stringed instrument and going round the room, beholding all the artistic designs.

Rama stepped forward and eulogised Narada. Narada uttered many words of blessings to Rama.

"Great Sage, you love your devotees. That's why you have appeared here to bless me on this auspicious occasion."

"The real lover of His devotees is Shri Narayana, Rama!"said Narada. "We simply link the rings of His divine activities."

"Lucky are those who have been entrusted with the work of linking rings by Shri Narayana," said Rama in a jovial mood. He added, "Great Sage! Whatever you deem fit for me, speak out. I need your blessings and guidance."

"Rama! You had made a promise to Vishwamitra," said Narada. Then he paused and looked at Rama.

Rama also looked at Narada. He was surprised to hear how Narada knew about his word given to Vishwamitra. Then, all of a sudden, he understood that Narada was always on the move. There might have been an accidental meeting with Vishwamitra also. The public opinion about him is that no place is inaccessible for the Sage Narada. He can emerge anywhere he likes.

"Great Sage! I remember my word. I had told him that I destroy all the demons of the earth and set up 'Satyuga' here," Rama emphasized his statement.

"Then Rama!" Narada cast his deep looks upon Rama," What will happen to your life's aim?"

"My lord! The cycle of fate is running. Whatever is good for all will happen. I've surrendered all the incidents of life to the destiny. Whatever destiny wants me to do, it will make it feasible for me to do. I am only a puppet."

"But Rama, do you think you will be able to fulfill your promise while holding the position of the king?" asked Narada with curiosity.

"Great Sage, it all depends on the will power of the king. Only that the will power of administration doesn't match with it. If the king resolves to put an end to injustice, cruelty and immorality, then the anti-social and immoral elements also understand that the time has come for them to follow in the righteous path."

"Yes, this is what I have heard and seen that it is the age of truth in Ayodhya under your leadership," said Narada. He continued, "The place where the king is good and morality-prone, has the age of truth automatically. But the place where the king is immoral and cruel becomes the centre of 'Kaliyug'. But how can it be that the age of truth prevails only in Ayodhya and the rest part of the earth is accursed with 'Kaliyug'? Then it will be as if the sun illumines only Ayodhya with its light and the remaining earth is affiliated with darkness and fear."

"But, the great sage, it doesn't lie within the nature of the sun. The Sun-god is far from prejudice. He gives light to all equally."

"This is what I am saying, Rama!" laughed Narada. "You are today's Sun, belonging to the Sun-dynasty. Sun-like Rama! It's everybody's wish that the light of the age of truth spreads everywhere. The heat of your sun scorches the evil beings and gives energy to the good people. But it's not possible as long as the demons' army is in and around all forests. See Ravana, who had been setting up his cantonments throughout the world though he rules over 'Lanka'. He is slowly progressing ahead. There is concentration of demon armies with their full might in every forest."

"Great Sage, Gurudeva Vishwamitra had described common masses' woes not only in words but he had also made me travel on foot to realize their sufferings. I have vowed to liberate this earth from all demons."

"Amen, Rama!" Narada felt assured of Rama's self-confidence.

After Narada's departure, Rama began to contemplate why the great sage was doubtful that I wouldn't be able to do my work freely if I remained glued to the king's throne. Most probably, his doubt was based on other king's behaviour. But if all the kings got united, the terror created by demons could be ended. I'll make all efforts to unite all the kings and masses to counter demons unflinchingly.

* * *

14

Manthara was gasping with greater intensity. Since she was hunch-backed, she had to spend more energy to walk fast. As she was heading towards Kaikeyi's palace, so was her balance of body getting upset. Like a monkey she was taking the support of her hands to climb high stairs of the palace's premises. When the other maid-servants saw the miserable condition of Manthara, they thought it better to greet her silently. They knew very well that if anybody said anything or if anyone fell on the way of the annoyed Manthara, she would have to suffer in one way or the other. It was quite certain.

She pushed open the doors of Kaikeyi's chamber, went inside and saw that she was lying with a netted stole covering her beautiful and happy face.

"Stupid! Rise up! Are you sleeping?" shrieked Manthara. Her whole body was shaking with extreme anger.

Kaikeyi opened her eyes indolently, yawned and looked at Manthara smilingly. Perhaps, it seemed, she didn't hear Manthara's furious and stern voice or didn't pay any attention to her severe and undignified language knowingly because she was familiar with her nature and too much freedom given to her.

Kaikeyi spoke," Manthrey! Today I have been in an ecstatic mood since morning. But I see no clear, perspicuous reason of it. I feel the currents of joy rising in my heart. My mind is absorbed in music and so my fingers are dancing on the veena."

"When you come to know that you're in the sea of troubles and that you're going to fall prey to a series of woes, all your joy will disappear into nothingness like camphor. The star of your ill-luck has risen, Kaikeyi!"

This time Kaikeyi read Manthara's mental state carefully. She saw that Manthara was like an idol of terrible anger and she was heaving very badly. She knew that Manthara was addicted to making a mountain out of a mole-hill now and then. Kaikeyi had been conversant with her temperament since her childhood. Her own mother had already bidden good-bye to this world. It was Manthara who had nursed her like a mother. She proved to be Kaikeyi's caretaker more than her mother. When Dashratha married Kaikeyi, Manthara thought that her life was dry and colourless. Then she expressed her desire to accompany Kaikeyi. Kaikeyi too gave her full regards though she was a mere maid-servant of hers. Manthara knew that she could talk with Kaikeyi fearlessly, that she could guide her. If she went against Manthara even a little bit, she would create a scene of hell. Manthara always kept in her mind what food would be suitable for Kaikeyi and what not, in what season she was to go out and when she was to stay in the palace, etc. A few days after arriving at Ayodhya, Manthara had proved by her conduct in the inner chamber of Kaikeyi that her instructions would be of supreme importance. Other maid-servants had understood Manthara's importance very soon.

Many times Kaikeyi felt hurt when Manthara used her acid tongue. But she never questioned Manthara, thinking that she had surrendered her whole life for her well-being. She thought that the faults of such a faithful woman were pardonable. Though Manthara was on the threshold of her old age yet there was no change in her nature of shouting and screaming. When she gave birth to Bharata, Manthara told her that priority would now be given to Bharata, and not to her. She gave clear instructions that she would not brook anyone's interference in respect of Bharata. Kaikeyi even went to the extent of saying smilingly that Manthara was after all Bharata's grandmother. Who could now bear the sharp-edged arrows of words of an out-spoken grandma? It actually happened so in real life. She took great care of all comforts and pleasures of Bharata like real grandmother. Even Kaikeyi couldn't know when Bharata grew young. She knew not if she had ever bathed or patted Bharata like a mother. She remembered only Rama because he spent more time with her rather than with Kausalya. In the beginning, of course, did she vex Rama out of ill-will. But God knows when she set her heart upon Rama. As she saw Rama, she was overbrimmed with motherly love for him. Whenever Rama called her 'Ma' or 'Maatey', it would shake her whole body with joy. No doubt, many times she scolded Rama but he never had any bad feeling for her in his heart. He would run to her and fall into her lap. Manthara had never seen anybody else but Bharata. No doubt, she had developed some affection for Shatrughana. But it was because Shatrughana was ever ready to lay down his life for Bharata. Manthara had begun to feel that only Shatrughana could take full care of Bharata in her absence. It was already in Shatrughana's heart yet by her untiring efforts she had made Shatrughana realize that he should stay loyal to Bharata. That's why she always encouraged Shatrughana to be in the company of Bharata. Though Manthara did not disregard Rama and Lakshmana yet she never gave them importance. She always took Rama to be Kaikeyi's plaything. She felt that if Kaikeyi didn't remain obsessed with Rama, she (Kaikeyi) would feel attracted towards Bharata and then it was possible that her hold on Bharata would become less.

"Mantharey!" Controlling her anger rising in her heart, Kaikeyi said," Someone must have uttered some unpleasant words to you. You're like a ripe crop. If anybody says to you unpleasant words, they work like fire. You burn yourself in that fire. Anyhow, I have seen you in this flaring condition after a long time."

"Just express your thoughts about Dashratha." Manthara looked askance, jerked her fingers and mouthed at Kaikeyi.

"My beloved husband! My beloved who is ever ready to lay down his life for me!" Kaikeyi sang it in the form of an amorous song.

"I knew this memorised song of yours. I knew you would sing it in response. But now you should try to understand," Manthara sat by the netted window after climbing two or three steps, "that Dashratha is going to take your life. When he comes before you, he poses as if he had surrendered everything of his to you. But behind your back he disregards you. He doesn't want your welfare. On the other hand, it is you who feel proud of him, taking him to be immersed in your love. Just as the river water evaporates in summer, in the same way, waves of Dashratha's love have dried up."

Kaikeyi felt hurt when she heard all this about Dashratha. Once she thought of reprimanding Manthara for using indecent and inappropriate language and tone for the Maharaja. But then she kept mum, thinking that Manthara used reverential words for Dashratha in public. Only when she was before her, she conducted herself like that as if she were truly his mother-in-law and she had a right to use stern words for her son-in-law.

"Manthara!" said Kaikeyi in her love-lorn voice, "See, today I'm extremely happy for no apparent reason. But you never get angry without any reason. Tell me why you're flaring up."

"Just peep out of the palatial chamber or see from the terrace how the entire Ayodhya had been adorned like a newly-wed bride in the twinkling of an eye. Such a kind of decoration had not been done even at the time of Bharata's wedding. Kaushlya's palace is decorated with earthen lamps. Her maid-servants are clad in silk dresses and stupid citizens of Ayodhya have spent their own money on decorating their houses. It looks as if it were the coronation of their sons, instead of Rama, the crown prince."

"What did you say? It's Rama's coronation!" leapt Kaikeyi out of joy. She moved forward speedily and helped sitting Manthara rise up. She swirled her and said, "Stupid! Does such good news ever frighten a person in such a dramatic fashion?"

"Leave me, will you make me fall?" Manthara released her hands from her hold. She sat on a stool and kept on looking at dancing Kaikeyi.

Dancingly Kaikeyi said to Manthara, "I was thinking my joy knew no reason. But if rain falls anywhere, only then can we breathe in the fragrance of soil. I was in the grip of the currents of this good news. Take this, Mantharey!"

Dancing Kaikeyi removed the priceless necklace from her neck and dropped it in Manthara's lap. She added," I am extremely happy with you. Beg, what you want in return for this good news. Mantharey! It is the sweetest and most pleasant news that you have conveyed to me in your life. The news of Rama's coronation is like nectar for me. You can ask for anything you like. Today I feel like giving away everything of mine to you."

"Then listen!" Holding the dancing Kaikeyi's hand and checking her with her terrible eyes and angry voice, Manthara said, "Sit by me for sometime and listen to me. This is what I want. If you are in woe, I'm woeful. And if you are in weal, I'm happy. You know it very well. But if you want to drink poison, taking it to be nectar, I will not let you do it." She threw away the necklace gifted to her by Kaikeyi and said, "This ornament is like a serpent for me. I am terribly vexed to see the imminent danger approaching you. I am astonished as well as aggrieved at your stupidity."

Kaikeyi felt that it was not an acting on the part of Manthara as she had taken it before. She is angry and furious in reality. Kaikeyi sat by Manthara in a very bad mood.

"Step-son is an enemy. The woman who is happy at the rise of her step-son can't be called wise,"said Manthara. "I fear Bharata will be the victim of Rama's conspiracy. Both have equal claim upon this kingdom. From the view-point of birth, it is Bharata who has a right to rule over this kingdom after Rama. It is certain that Rama will cast away Bharata like a thorn from his life."

"What nonsense are you talking, Manthara?" said Kaikeyi, feeling aggreived. "Do you think Bharata will be like a thorn in Rama's eyes, and not Lakshmana and Shatrughana? Are they his real brothers?"

"They may not be his real brothers but they are not his rivals," said Manthara. You are totally ignorant about politics as well as diplomacy. You don't know Rama. He has full knowledge of all scriptures and is adept in warfare. He knows how to destroy his enemy that comes in his way. This is what politics and principles based on experience say. So, Rama is thinking upon all these possibilities."

"How can you say so? What proof do you have to support your statement?" Kaikeyi said with severity.

"You want proof! My goodness!" Manthara beat her breast, "O God, Why have you made my Kaikeyi so simple and sinless? Why did you not give her even ordinary intelligence to see through the event that was going against her welfare?"

She turned towards Kaikeyi, "If an area is sun-lit and if someone asks for the proof of the presence of the Sun-god in the sky, what will you say? You want proof! Can't you see that Rama sent Bharata to your father's house so that in his absence he may have his coronation?"

"Rama hasn't sent Bharata to my father's house,"explained Kaikeyi. My brother had come to take him. It's not the first time that Bharata has gone to his grandfather's house. He often goes there. This news might have already been sent to Bharata. He will come."

"You say he will come!" Manthara laughed sarcastically. "Tomorrow morning under the holy stars the most scholarly brahmins will coronate Shri Rama, the son of that fortunate Kausalya. She will get the kingdom on this earth because she is the most trustworthy chief queen of Maharaja Dashratha. You are now going to be her maid-servant who will stand in her service with folded hands and Bharata, king Rama's servant."

"O hunch-backed!" smiled Kaikeyi. She added, "Simple-minded I am not but you who are thinking of inauspicious things by accusing Rama of conspiracies of different kingdoms. Rama knows not only of politics but also of religion. He is holy and truthful. Since he is the eldest son of the Maharaja, he is the legitimate claimant of being the Crown Prince. May he live long! He will be the affectionate care-taker of his brothers by virtue of his father's command. O hunch-backed! Why are you feeling vexed so much on knowing about Shri Rama's coronation? Why are you overbrimmed with jealously? This is a grand event in which lies the well-being of all. Why do you seek ungood in it and feel troubled? For me Rama is many-fold greater than Bharata. You never let Bharata come to me. There has always been a distance between both of us. But Rama clings to me as if I were his mother. If Rama is getting the kingdom, it means that it automatically belongs to Bharata. It's because Rama is never prejudicial in his behaviour towards his brothers. But I feel that he showers his love upon his younger brothers as if they were his sons."

Manthara breathed in deeply and said, "It's rightly written in scriptures that when bad time comes, man loses his wit. For him even inauspicious things look auspicious. The same is happening to you. You were born in the royal family. You are the great queen of the great king. You ought to have knowledge of politics and cruelty. Your husband always talks with you about religion and polity, but in reality, he is a liar. He uses his confectionate and affectionate words while talking with you, but at heart he is atrocious. You have always thought that he loves you and he expresses his feelings with good intention, and you have let yourself being gulled by him."

"Manthara, bid good-bye to your hatred and ill-will! Tell me on what grounds you are blaming him. I have never heard the Maharaja tell a lie. He has never been seen doing any ungood or playing any bad politics," said Kaikeyi.

"Kaikeyi, you are talking of 'grounds'! It is before you. The only thing is that you are not trying to see it. This is a bad luck of yours and mine as well." said Manthara in angry excitement. "He is putting the entire wealth of the state in the lap of Kausalya. And it is you who don't happen to see his partiality. He has already sent Bharata to your father's house. Tomorrow morning he will, all of a sudden, hand over the kingdom to Rama without any hindrance. Can't you see this polluted politics of his? Bharata's maternal uncle, Yudhajita is a wise and sensible man. As soon as he gets the news that Rama's coronation has occurred, he won't send Bharata back to Ayodhya, thinking that his life will be unsafe. Why don't you understand the gravity of the situation? Your condition is like that of a person who nurtures a serpent in his sleeve as he is blind in love, and then the same snake bites him one day. Similarly, you gave place to the Maharaja in your lap and he like a snake behaved with you."

"Go on speaking, Mantharey!" smiled Kaikeyi.

"Keykaya Princess! Even after hearing such awful and inauspicious words from me, you're looking at me with joyous surprise as if I am an ignorant child and you are enjoying my silly, stupid talks. If you didn't forsake your excessive love for the Maharaja, you would be in lurch. I, therefore want you to perform such an act quickly that you find yourself, Bharata and me safe."

"Why will Rama do any harm to Bharata, me and you? said Kaikeyi to Manthara scoldingly. "Do you have any evidence to produce that goes to prove that Rama or the Maharaja intends to harm us?"

"This sort of diplomacy is beyond your understanding, Keykaya Princess!" laughed Manthara. "This is what I am going to make you understand for such a long time. After Rama, his son will be the king and Bharata will be detached from inheritance. Like an orphan, he will be deprived of all his pleasures and comforts of life. Most of the time of his childhood Bharata spent in his grandmother's house. This is the only reason why he is not in favour of the Maharaja. It is but natural that whosoever lives with us, we begin to love him. If Bharata had been brought up here, the Maharaja must have handed him his entire kingdom. If not entire, he must have handed him over half of his kingdom."

"Whatever you are saying is all against the rules. In a kingdom, the eldest son of a king is entitled to be the king after his father's death. It is only when he is incapable, other sons are taken into consideration." said Kaikeyi.

"But after giving a word this tradition has no meaning," smiled Manthara cruelly. "Maharaja Dashratha is bound by the word given to king Keykaya. Only on the basis of his word, he had given his daughter in marriage to Maharaja Dashratha that the son born to his daughter would inherit Ayodhya, and this word had been given by nobody else but amorous Dashratha."

"It was just an ordinary word of laughter and amusement," said Kaikeyi.

"No!" shrieked Manthara. "It's the tradition of Raghu dynasty that they never tell a lie even in their dreams. Every word uttered by them is in itself a proof. If even Shatrughana had been present here, he would have immediately stopped this unjust occurrence. Just as Lakshmana is always ready to protect Rama, similarly, Shatrughana too always thinks of the welfare of Bharata and is devoted to him. This is the reason why even Shatrughana was sent with Bharata so that there might be no possibility of any rising hindrance."

But it was all beyond Kaikeyi's understanding. She held her brow with her hand and sat up on her bed.

"You know it very well that when you came to Ayodhya as a newly wed bride, you left no stone unturned to torment Kausalya with a view to end her influence in the palace. But Kausalya was then silent, and you thought that she would no longer be a thorn in your way, you stopped vexing her. You felt that it was your high handedness to have done so. But now her son will be the king. She will be as powerful as you were then. Even the Maharaja will be under her thumb and then she will take revenge upon you slowly and steadily. Give a serious thought to it. We are not left with much time to think upon it. Think out of such a plan that Rama is straightaway sent to the forest and Bharata sits on the throne. This is what was Maharaja's word."

Kaikeyi visualised the time when she had vexed Kausalya and Rama in order to establish her supremacy over them. She remembered how she had spat her ill-will and malice upon them. If the same thing had been done with her, she would have naturally taken revenge immediately after gaining power. And so far as Maharaja Dashratha is concerned...! Manthara is right when she says that he showers his love upon me but wealth upon Kausalya. If he was intent upon coronating Rama, he should have taken me into his confidence. He should have at least given me its information. But he didn't do so. After all, what was the urgency that obliged him to take this quick decision within one night? Yes, it may be that Bharata, when he returns home, remains silent because he looks upon Rama as his ideal father and stands before him with his bowed head. It may be a part of their policies to keep Bharata under control. Manthara is right to say that since Shatrughana will oppose their move and his protest will be construed as Bharata's protestations, a conspiracy will be hatched to quell the uprising. When Kaikeyi thought this, she shivered from within. She said to herself, 'I had never thought of it. Nor had I ever seen through their tricks. And how I could think and see when Rama and Kausalya had touched me with their wand of love!'

Kaikeyi's mind at once changed. Her face turned red in anger. Her breaths became hot and fast. Her heart that was some time ago was an aquarium of love and joy turned into a pond of poison. She began to see all that Manthara wanted her to see. She began to think, 'If Rama becomes the king of Ayodhya, Bharata will be jilted and insulted from time to time. Rama will never give him a suitable post in the royal assembly. Bharata will always be pushed into the jaws of death by sending him to fight the slaves and the demons. My own life will not be better than that of a maid servant.'

Then she thought of the other side of the picture, 'If Bharata is made the king and Rama is exiled, Bharata will become as popular as Rama is. People will then hail him. But the question is why Rama will be banished. Dashratha had simply talked about making my son the king of Ayodhya and there was no hint about exiling Rama or sending all his remaining sons to a forest. In such a situation, Rama will naturally protest against Bharata. At present, all the military powers vest with Rama.' Kaikeyi, puffed up with anger, felt desperate. She thought of scratching Dashratha's face and asking him what had happened to his word of promise.

Again, she lapsed into her evil thoughts, 'It seems that that promise has lost its weightage and importance. If I or my parents had kept reminding Dashratha of his promise, this critical situation wouldn't have risen. The entire subject, army, council of ministers, etc. would have been ready for this. How did I forget this important thing and how did my parents also forget totally about it? Did all of them take his word in a light vein?'

'Kaikeyi, what nonsense are you thinking of?' echoed her inner voice. 'Don't put salt of jealousy and hatred into the milk of love. Don't allow your maid-servant who is physically and mentally mutilated to sway over you. You're thinking sinfully. At present, you enjoy an honourable status. On her instigation, if you express your narrow and sinful thoughts, do you know what will happen? It is certain that Bharata will not be the king of Ayodhya. You too will lose your prestige and honour.'

'But if Rama is made the king, I'll get destroyed. And with me, even Bharata.' She pounced upon her inner voice in the same way as a lioness does upon an animal that moves forward towards her target.

When that voice saw the terrible from of Kaikeyi, it became silent. Kaikeyi now turned towards Manthara and said, "You're very right, O hunch-backed! Rama must be exiled and Bharata must be the king of Ayodhya. But how can this impossible task be made possible? Now time has slipped out of our hands."

"My daughter!" Passing her hand on Kaikeyi's head, Manthara said affectionately, " How can you say that time has gone? The coronation of Rama hasn't yet taken place. The whole night and tomorrow morning are at our disposal."

"But take it for granted that this time has also passed," said Kaikeyi desperately.

"No, my grand queen! Trust me. If you act upon my advice, Bharata will certainly be the king of Ayodhya and Rama shall be banished."

"How?" screamed Kaikeyi.

"By virtue of boons?" said Manthara calmly. Her eyes were assessing Kaikeyi's mental state and she was influencing her with the cycle of her evil thoughts. Making her voice ambiguous, she said, "Recollect the day when at the end of the war between gods and demons, the Maharaja, in return for your unprecedented contribution, had begged you to ask for her two boons. You had told him that when she desired so, she would ask for them. You yourself had told me this and now you've definitely forgotten this. But I haven't. I've always carried it in my mind. Now the time has come to ask for them, Kaikeyi!"

"Yes, Maharaja had granted me two boons."

"Then today, on the strength of those boons, you should make impossible possible,"shouted Manthara out of joy. "The first boon should be about Bharata to be made the king of Ayodhya and the second boon about Rama to be banished for fourteen years."

"Fourteen years?" Kaikeyi's forehead was creased with lines of queries.

"Yes, fourteen years. Because by that time Bharata will be able to control Ayodhya and he will become the heart-throb of Ayodhya's people. In the forests the demon army is ready to hunt for Rama. While fighting against the demons, Rama will be killed. But if Rama becomes the king, Bharata will be sent on war campaign against the demons."

"But why is demon army so much excited about Rama?"

"Forgetting things is your habit, Kaikeyi! Don't you remember that Vishwamitra had killed Tadaka and her sons with the assistance of Rama and Lakshmana? You know very well how powerful and revengeful the demons are. Banishment will put an end to Rama," said Manthara.

She continued, "Take advantage of this golden opportunity. Put on your dirty clothes. Go to your chamber and reveal your resentment. Scatter all your ornaments here and there and lie down on the ground. When Dashratha comes to you, neither look at him nor talk to him. You simply act like a terrible fish and lament. So far as my experience of life goes, Maharaja Dashratha loves you the most. If he finds you in woe, he can even jump into the fire. You are his heart throb and he is always ready to fulfil every desire of yours. He can even lay his life down for you. Kaikeyi, recognize the might of your good luck!" Manthara rested for breath. Then she continued, "Maharaja will try to offer you various temptations in order to please you. But you should reject them all and remind him only of those two boons. Then he will at once get ready to fulfil them. When the Maharaja helps you rise up with his hands and embraces you, you should again remind him of the veracity of boons and ask for those two boons to be fulfilled by him."

"Manthara! The world says that the hunch-backed are sinners. Their soul is immersed in sins. But you are an exception. You are not a sinner. If you hadn't been with me, I would never have discovered Rama's conspiracy. Though you are hunch-backed, your whole personality is beautiful. You are my true benefactress. As soon as Bharata becomes the king, you will be loaded with ornaments studded with gems. You will be most influential in Ayodhya. You are really well- versed in politics and diplomacy. I don't know why I couldn't identify you by this time."

"Kaikeyi, don't waste your time in useless talks," there was a warning in Manthara's voice. "If crops die, rain is of no avail. If Rama's coronation is over, these two boons will become fruitless. At the moment I am not thinking of wealth, food and clothes. If Rama's coronation takes place, the Maharaja will get the news of my death. Now my life rests on only one thing. The thing is that Bharata should be Ayodhya's king and Rama should be banished for fourteen years."

× × ×

After Kaikeyi's departure for her chamber, Manthara heaved a sigh of relief. She had laboured hard to wipe out the imprint of Rama and Kaushalya's love from the heart and soul of Kaikeyi. Now she was very tired. Even then the feeling that her diplomacy would show its best results removed her tiredness.

'Manthara! What have you done?' asked her inner soul.

'What good will come out of asking this question now? Why didn't you ask when I was trying my best to change Kaikeyi's mind?' laughed Manthara.

'Then my voice was submerged in the ocean of the noise of your hatred. Now your sinful voice is quiet and so you're in a position to hear my cricket-like sound of voice.'

'For my safety and domination,' laughed Manthara like a conqueror.

'If Rama had become the king, do you think he would have killed you and Bharata? Would he have robbed you of your domination?' asked the voice.

'Never. There is no violence in Rama's nature. This is the reason why I talked about his fourteen years of banishment. He can be happy in every condition, but I can't. I found out that under the orders of Vishwamitra Rama had lived and walked on foot like forest dwellers and that he had picked up dry leaves and pieces of wood. Both the brothers had to sleep on ground covered with grass and dry leaves, and they thanked their stars for this. Rama had even made a promise to Vishwamitra that again he would come back to the forests to kill the demons. My soul! If you consider this matter seriously, you'll find that nobody else is a protectress of the religion so much as Manthara is.'

'You and the protectress of religion?' said her voice.

'Yes, I'm the protectress of religion!' There was a tinge of self-pride in Manthara's voice. She said, 'This action of mine will increase the prestige of Raghu dynasty. The whole world will admire them that they give more importance to their word than to their life. They never allow any situation to stand as a stumbling block in the way of fulfilling their promises. Now all the promises will be fulfilled- the one given by Rama to Vishwamitra, the one given by Dashratha to Kakaya king long back and now the ones given by Dashratha to Kaikeyi. After these promises are fulfilled the rein of administration of Ayodhya will be in my hands. The whole world will see and know that a hunch-backed woman who was jured at and jilted because of her physical disability can change the world map by dint of her intelligence.'

'The world will only spit on you for your misdeed.'

On hearing her inner voice, Manthara laughed like a mad person. When her laughter stopped she said, 'When you are powerful, the world doesn't spit on you but worships you. Might is worshiped. The world salutes the influential. All these people who are eulogising Rama today will sing songs of praise in Bharata's honour and dignity when he becomes the king. The very same people will bow their heads before Bharata and will thank their stars. This same physically mutilated hunch-backed woman will rule over all those who are considered to be innocent and good-looking physically.'

'Everything was going on smoothly well. Why are you falling upon Ayodhya like a meteor?' said the voice.

'Some time back even Dashratha had fallen upon Keykaya kingdom like a meteor. By way of compensation, the king of Keykaya kingdom had given his young daughter in marriage to Dashratha who was on the verge of old age. How can I forget that juncture?' When Manthara recollected that time, she got excited, 'Then the king of Keykaya kingdom and his ministers had asked Kaikeyi what she could do to safeguard the interests of her country. She had then replied that she could even sacrifice her life for the country. And she practically did what she had said. Dashratha was extremely happy to marry her. She had offered herself to the fire of yajna.'

'Manthara, if it is so, what troubles you then?' said the voice. It continued, 'Those who were its victim forgot its pain. Did Kaikeyi ever make a complaining cry?'

'Kaikeyi will never do so because she had offered herself to the yajna fire.'

'Did the king of Keykaya kingdom ever make a protest?'

'He is under the suzerainty of king Dashratha.'

'Then what are you? You are an ordinary maid-servant. You are a hunch-backed woman,' scolded the voice. It continued, 'You act as if you were the queen. Don't you feel ashamed of destroying the kingdom that gave you shelter? And that too without any rhyme or reason. If you had been the victim of injustice, cruelty and insult and if you had been disregarded and tormented, one could have justified your evil move. But this cruel conduct of yours towards these simple royal personage!'

'Intentionally I corrupted Kaikeyi's mind. I had thrown only my dice and it acted according to my wish. The rest part of the game will be in my hands.' When Manthara laughed boisterously, it seemed that the walls of the palace would collapse. She continued, 'I had no hope that Kaikeyi would be under the influence of my magic mantra. But when I told her how Kaushalya could take revenge upon her and how Bharata's life would be at stake, Kaikeyi fell prey to me. I don't know what's going on my mind. But as I imagine of Dashratha feeling helpless and hopeless, I experience inner peace and joy. The very notion that the great king of Ayodhya is lying on the ground lifelessly, helplessly, and desperately, and his past glory and grandeur is like a dream for him, makes me dance with joy.'

'O hunch-backed woman! You are handicapped not only physically but mentally also,' scolded the voice.

Manthara continued to laugh like mad persons.

'YOU are a sinner and a psychopath.'

Manthara began to dance like a crazy person.

The voice became quiet.

* * *

15

Dashratha felt happy and took in deep breath. He stood before the mirror. He saw his own refection and felt that he was looking somewhat young. Though there were many signs of old age on his body and especially on his face yet something kept him young from within. 'Why Dashratha! He called his own image in the mirror. 'Who will be more fortunate than you today? You were unnecessarily worried about Rama's coronation how it would be arranged in such a short time? Was there any obstacle anywhere? Any bad omens? You get scared so easily. Look, as you get worried, old age begins to show its signs. And when you are happy, you begin to look young and live-wire. Say, what do you think now?'

Dashratha turned his ear towards his reflection as if he were going to hear something, 'What did you say? Do you want to go to ladies' chamber? To inform with your own mouth about Rama's abrupt coronation... What did you say? You will first go to Kaikeyi? I knew you got utmost happiness from the love-play with her. It is because she is junior to you in age. She is still young in comparison with you. Yes, yes! Go! Enjoy your royal self to the fullest.'

Dashratha was in a very happy mood when he turned towards Kaikeyi's chamber. He ordered the charioteer to drive the chariot.

'Dashratha!' said his inner voice, ' You should have gone for another marriage.'

' You've come to tease me,' laughed Dashratha.

'It's a matter of happiness and not an act of teasing,' laughed the voice. 'Just think if there had been another queen younger than Kaikeyi!'

'Look here, I know you're playing with me. I can't be under your control and can't imagine of unnecessary things. Kaikeyi alone is enough for my amusement and recreation. Now my Rama will bring more princesses for himself.'

'How much do you know about Rama, Dashratha?' It looked as if the voice pinched Dashratha and disappeared.

All of a sudden, Dashratha's fury shook his whole body. When his pain eased, he thought, 'This Rama too! The more I tried to understand him, the more complicated he became for me; I could never know or understand him. He is a prince but mundane pleasures of life don't even touch him. Many times it seemed as if an ascetic's soul had enshrined itself in him. The princes of his age otherwise dip in the river of pleasures of life; plunge into the rivers of alcoholic drinks. But Rama is indifferent towards royal pleasures. No news of his love-affair with anyone, no public comments. He was neither seen nor heard of spending the night at any dancer's place. If you peep into his eyes, you will find no trace of lust in them. He is devoted to only one spouse. Which king keeps only one queen? If a king has upteen queens and sub-queens, he is regarded as powerful.'

'As you are powerful!' said that voice as if hidden in the cave.

' You continue your absurd talks. I am not listening to you,' laughed Dashratha.

'You are listening to me. That's why you are answering me,' laughed the voice louder than Dashratha.

Dashratha felt bitterness in his mouth. He directed his mind towards his pensive thoughts, 'These brothers of Rama! For them Rama is a model. They are his shadows. They follow in his footsteps. There is neither adornment nor attraction of any kind in their life. They are only conscious of their duties. Service, austerity, mercy, pity, kindness, love are the qualities of the rishis and munis. Does a yajna performed for a son yield divine sons?'

'If you think of it properly, it is good for you,' said the voice that stood before him unexpectedly.

'How is it good for me?' Dashratha opened his mouth.

'If any evil spirit had taken the shape of your sons, your life would have become a hell. The internal strife between father and son would have over-shadowed the state council. You would have suffered from a phobia thinking that your son might not deprive you of your kingdom or imprison you or kill you by deceitful means. What do you say about it?'

'Why did you come to frighten me at this most opportune time?' Dashratha gulped down.

'Oh! The Maharaja is frightened. I seek your pardon, Maharaja! It doesn't behove Shri Rama's father to be scared,' laughed the voice.

As soon as Dashratha heard the name 'Rama' his mind was filled with peace.

"Maharaja!" called the charioteer.

Dashratha woke up as if from sleep. He saw that the chariot stood before Kaikeyi's palace, and the charioteer as well as his body guards waited for him to step down. Dashratha felt ashamed of himself. He didn't know how long the chariot stood there. He felt that his servants might have noticed the ups and downs of his feelings on his face. They might have murmured something and his bodyguards might have been laughing within their sleeves on seeing his age-worn condition.

"Oh! I dozed off to sleep." Dashratha yawned and stepped down the chariot quickly. Without looking at anybody, he said, "All of you should celebrate tonight."

Dashratha was climbing up the compound's steps as if he were a young prince. His lips were moving. He was full of zeal and zest. He was imagining that when Kaikeyi saw him in such an exalted mood, she would shower upon him her boundless love. Nature was at her best in the palace. The peacocks were making a piercing cry. It seemed as if Kaikeyi were calling him through them. Parrots, geese, etc. were making the whole complex musical with their notes. They were better accompained by various musical instruments. There were Champa and Ashoka trees all around. It appeared as if they were fanning Dashratha's love-lorn feelings and the murals on the walls were also contributing their share. There were many dwarf-sized and hunch-backed maid-servants who were running pell mell. On seeing them, Dashratha laughed. Their sight reminded him of the time when Kaikeyi had entered the palace as a newly-wed queen. Only after a few days, all the beautiful maids had been retrenched from the chamber. They were superceded by many hunch-backed and pigmy-sized maid-servants. When Dashratha asked Kaikeyi its reason, he was told that the so-called Manthara, her personal maid-servant, was a hunch-backed woman and it was the ardent desire of Manthara that other dwarf-sized and hunch-backed women should get an opportunity to serve the palace. But Sumantra had another reason to tell. He had concluded that in front of beautiful women, Manthara was deeply conscious of her physical deformity. She always suffered from inferiority complex. If anyone laughed for any other reason, she felt that she was being laughed at. Hence, she is at ease in the midst of other hunch-backed and pigmy-sized maid-servants. She keeps her control over them.

Dashratha entered Kaikeyi's chamber in an ecstatic mood. He saw that Kaikeyi was not in her bed. He thought that she was perhaps playing with him the hide and seek game. He thought it could not be that she didn't get any news of his approach.

As his chariot turns towards the road leading to Kaikeyi's inner chamber, all the security guards sitting on the roof top convey the news of his arrival. And in no time the already adorned palace is decorated more.

"Kaikeyi!" called out Dashratha.

"My lady!"

"My Heart!"

"My Benefactress!"

"O Beloved Better-half!"

But all his addresses proved to be futile. This was the first time of his life when Kaikeyi was not before his eyes on his arrival. She had never played the hide and seek game with him before this. He was vexed to think so. He was so much obsessed with love for Kaikeyi that he wanted to fall into her lap at the earliest. He thought of taking full rest in the shade of Kaikeyi's love.

He turned his attention towards the chamber again. There was a strange kind of calmness. On his arrival, the maid-servants sitting outside her chamber used to charge the whole complex with musical notes by playing Veena, drums and flutes. They offered him garlands and fragrant bunches of flowers. But today it was absent. The question arose in Dashratha's mind whether Kaikeyi was off-colour.

Dashratha hurriedly came out of her chamber. A maid-servant came in sight. She began to tremble with fear. She folded her hands, touched her forehead with them and said in her shaken voice, "May Lord pardon me!"

"Where is the Chief Queen Kaikeyi?" asked Dashratha in his vexed voice.

"On hearing the news of your arrival, she became furious and has now run into her retiring chamber," the maid-servant bowed her head after saying so. Dashratha thought of asking her if Kaikeyi should have gone into her retiring chamber on learning about his arrival or why Kaikeyi had gone there, etc. But then on second thought, the king felt that it would be indiscreet on his part to ask her. He stepped forward quickly towards the chamber. His whole attention was fixed on her words that Kaikeyi had run into her chamber in anger. It meant that the queen was either off-colour or angry with him. Dashratha's heart was full of grief. Now he began to think that he would have to first try his best efforts to appease her; only then he would be able to win her love. He said to himself, 'This woman-race! When a man is in need of her, only then a stumbling-block is created in the way of his rising energy. But the question is why Kaikeyi is furious with him. In her previous meeting with him she had thanked her stars for having got me as her husband. And today, all of a sudden, she feels as if she had been robbed of her wealth.'

When Dashratha got into her retiring chamber, he felt gulled. Kaikeyi was lying with her face down on the ground. She was wearing dirty clothes and her hair was dishevelled. It looked as if she had lost her way in a forest and was lying lifelessly. All the ornaments and other articles of the chamber were lying scattered here and there. It looked as if she had struggled hard in her self-defense. Dashratha moved towards Kaikeyi and sat by her. His heart was throbbing hard in doubt and fear. He feared that if he tried to touch Kaikeyi lovingly, she might not pounce upon him like a wounded lioness. So he thought it better to wait for a while. Another thought that she might not have been aware of his arrival came into his mind; she might be sleeping. He bent a little more to assess Kaikeyi's present condition. She was heaving slowly. Her breaths were deep, long and slow. Perhaps she was murmuring something. It seemed that Dashratha was going to lose his forbearance. At present he wished Kaikeyi to swing him in her lap out of love and sing amorous songs to amuse him. At last Dashratha advanced both of his hands towards her. He passed his one hand over her hair and the other hand over her back. Then he spoke to her in his amorous voice," My Love! I can't agree that you are angry with me. How can my beloved be angry with me? Tell me who has insulted you or obliged you to retire into your chamber out of grief. O my Benefactress! You know very well how vexed I am to see you in this plight. Then why are you dirtying your tender and beautiful body in the dust? O my spouse! I feel that some demon or ghost had taken you in his possession. If you are not well, then tell me, I will order the best physicians to cure you." Dashratha paused for a while. He was satisfied that Kaikeyi didn't react violently when he touched her.

Kaikeyi was feeling Dashratha's impulse of loving touch on her body. She felt a wave of joy in her heart. Simultaneously her inner voice spoke to her, 'O cruel! Why are you tormenting your lover? Just think what harm he has done to you! He has always loved and honoured you most of all his queens. He has always given importance to your desires and wishes. Not a single action of his can be pointed out that goes to prove that he has ever disregarded you. You cast your eyes upon yourself! See what you are doing. On this auspicious occasion when the whole Ayodhya is plunged in the ocean of joy, you are creating a gloomy atmosphere as if born out of death. Still there is time for you to rise up, throw your arms around his neck and embrace him. He will understand that you were only pretending to be so. It will fill him with extreme joy and will love you more than ever.'

When Kaikeyi imagined all this, she became happy.

As she was going to embrace Dashratha, she felt as if someone had held her tightly. She saw before her mental eye the sight of Manthara who was like a she-serpent, hissing wildly and looking at her with her red-hot eyes. Manthara shrieked, ' O Stupid! Use your wits. This heart of yours will make you a nonentity. If you act upon its advice, everything will end in smoke. I am simply a maid-servant. It makes no difference to me. But you will become a maid-servant and your son Bharata also will either become a menial servant or the food of demons. Mind if you act upon my advice, it will be contrary to it. Bharata will be Ayodhya's king, Kaushalya- a disregarded queen and Rama, a forest dweller, wandering from forest to forest in his attempt to save his life. Keep on lying in the same condition and torment Dashratha a little more.'

Dashratha felt that Kaikeyi was sobbing. "My love! Why are you making yourself ugly by weeping so bitterly? Tell me only once. I am ready to even kill the one who is forbidden to be killed. If there is any criminal who is to be hanged, tell me -I will set him free with honour. Or if any poor is to be made rich or rich poor, I'll do. I and my whole kingdom are waiting for your command. I am ready to fulfill every wish of yours. For this, I am prepared to forego my life. The only one thing that I want from you is that you shouldn't get angry with me. Be happy. You know my power. Dravida, Sindhu, Saueera, Swarashtra, South India, Anga, Banga, Maghda, Matsya, Kaashi, Kosal and many other prosperous countries are under my suzerainty. Whatever you want from me you can demand. I want to see you happy and healthy in every situation."

Kaikeyi was in doldrums. On the one hand her inner soul was asking to give up her anger and on the other Manthara was ready to beat it with a whip. Her inner soul said, 'Bid good-bye to your obstinacy. If you find Rama and Dashratha's conduct according to as Manthara says, you can tell Dashratha later to honour his promises. Then Bharata will be the King of Ayodhya and Rama will be exiled.'

Kaikeyi realized that her inner soul was right. Just then she saw Manthara making an assault on her inner soul. Manthara shrieked, 'Get away from here. You are bent upon throwing Kaikeyi into the pool of poverty.' Manthara turned towards Kaikeyi and said, 'If you don't act upon my advice you will repent later.'

'But what's wrong with this suggestion?'asked Kaikeyi.

'There is everything wrong in it.' said Manthara in anger. 'I don't know how many times I'll have to repeat the same thing. You Simpleton! When Rama becomes the king, Dashratha will have no right to remove him. Dashratha is still the king. The ways of the world are that as long as a man holds his post, he has his importance.' Manthara waved her whip in the air and lashed the queen's inner soul loudly.

Kaikeyi rose up. Her eyes were blood-like red. She took in deep, long and hot breath and looked at Dashratha. She spoke sternly, "My Lord! Who has got so much courage as to insult me? But I have got a burning ambition of life which you alone can fulfill it."

"Oh! This is only a trivial matter. You frightened me," Dashratha burst into wild laughter and kept on laughing. It seemed as if he were overshadowed by laughter.

Kaikeyi felt that she had perhaps made a mistake while playing her acting and that's why Dashratha was laughing ceaselessly.

"What is it that makes you laugh so much?" She made her voice sterner.

"It's only a laughable matter. You too laugh." Dashratha was laughing open-heartedly.

Kaikeyi realized that if she didn't keep control over her feelings, she would also begin to laugh. She tried to unhold herself from Dashratha. She jerked his hand and said, "I want something from you."

"Given everything," Dashratha kept on laughing. He didn't take it ill when Kaikeyi jerked his hand. He said lovingly, "My love! What did you see here between you and me? Everything is yours. I also belong to you. Don't demand, command me. You are the mistress. Be happy, my love!"

"No, until you take an oath and say you'll fulfill my heart-felt desire, I'll not be happy," said Kaikeyi in anger.

This made Dashratha a little bit serious. He held Kaikeyi by her hair with love. He kept her head in his lap and passing his hand on her forehead, said, "Kaikeyi! If anybody I love most after you, it is Rama. Nobody else do I love so much. It's by that Rama I say that I'll fulfill all your desires. I am at such a stage that if I don't see Rama even for a while, I begin to feel lifeless. I can sacrifice myself and all my other sons for the sake of Rama. So, you can demand whatever you want; I'll give you that."

Kaikeyi concentrated all her attention upon what Dashratha stated, 'I can sacrifice myself and all other sons for the sake of Rama. It means that if any necessity arises, he can remove even Bharata from Rama's path or that he will not prevent Rama from doing any harm to Bharata. Manthara is right when she says that I am unaware of the evil cycle of politics.'

"So it means you give me word!" Kaikeyi felt somewhat satisfied and acted as if she were happy.

"I give you word by my good deeds."

"Then listen, O King!" Kaikeyi laughed. Turning her face towards the sky and raising her hands up, she swung and said, "O Gods! O Moon, Sun, Nakshatras, Gandhara, Demons, Domestic Gods and many other moving and unmoving creatures! Listen to me. Maharaja Dashratha- the brave, truth loving, religious and noble- minded - is bound by his word given to his most loving Chief Queen, Kaikeyi." Placing her hands upon Dashratha's shoulders, she said, "O King! Recollect your promise given to me at the time of war between gods and demons." Dashratha's suspicious mind couldn't understand why he was being reminded of the war between gods and demons at that juncture. When he thought of it hard, he found that more than fifteen years had elapsed when that incident occurred; even two decades might have passed. He couldn't understand what lay hidden in that war between gods and demons that Kaikeyi's mind turned towards it and that she had retired into her chamber in anger. He remembered Lord Indra's words that if Dashratha hadn't come into his camp to help him, he would have lost his courage. Indra was besieged by demons and the gods were definitely going to lose the war. There was no such king as could seek enmity with the demons. Then there was no question of waging war against the demons. At that time Lord Indra sought the help of Dashratha who was chivalrous, truthful and religious-minded. Indra didn't expect that Dashratha would come to his help because a little time ago it was his third marriage with a very beautiful princess, Kaikeyi. In such a situation, no other king would have been ready to go to war and no council of ministers would have allowed the army to throw itself into somebody else's war. Even if the king had crossed all the bars, the royal family would have stood as a stumbling block. With such a state of mind Indra had sent his message to Dashratha to protect him. But he knew very well that it won't be 'Accepted'. But then

Indra's surprise knew no bounds when he saw Dashratha. Dashratha had accepted his invitation. He had arrived not only with his army but also with his newly-wed wife, Kaikeyi. Indra thought that Dashratha had perhaps come there to celebrate his honeymoon. Anyhow, Indra offered his gratitude to Dashratha and asked him the reason why Kaikeyi had accompanied him. Dashratha had told him that Kaikeyi put one condition before him. If she was not allowed to accompany him to see the war, she would not allow him to go to war for help. So, Dashratha felt that he would not accept any kind of impediment in the way of truth. If Kaikeyi wanted to accompany him, she could. He would not frustrate her. On hearing this, Indra's heart was full of thankfulness for Dashratha's virtues. The war started. Dashratha fought heroically. Kaikeyi, in the army uniform was sitting in the chariot. She was enjoying the war scene. Just then the arrows wounded Dashratha. He lost his consciousness. When he regained consciousness, he found himself in a camp. Kaikeyi and Indra were standing before him.

Indra had said, "Dashratha! I thought that your queen was only a soft-bodied woman but she was an amazon also. When you got wounded, she took you out of the battlefield quite safe and sound. She also fought so bravely that the enemies couldn't stand before her." Dashratha had taken her to be the incarnation of Durga. He was so confident and happy that he felt he could never pay off the debt of Kaikeyi who had saved his life and honour.

But now why she was thinking of that war, he couldn't understand. He failed to judge what was its connection with the war, which Kaikeyi was wishing to remind him of.

"O Benefactress! I remember all that. I remember that you had saved my life and the honour of my dynasty," said Dashratha in brief.

"And then you had out of joy told me to ask for two boons."

"Yes, I do remember," Dashratha opened his mouth.

"If you remember, then tell me what were those two boons." Kaikeyi's smile became evil. She felt that she was a successful actress.

"You..." Dashratha paused for a while and then said, "You hadn't asked for any boon. But you had said that in future if she needed them, she would ask for them."

"Today I feel their need. I want you to accomplish your boons as I had saved your life and dynasty's honour. I hope you are still bound by your word, Maharaja!" Kaikeyi peeped into Dashratha's vexed eyes. "Yes, I am bound by my word," said Dashratha firmly. But his voice was telling her that his firmness was apparent. From within he was feeling as if he were besieged by some inauspicious thing. He couldn't understand why Kaikeyi was making such a big background to ask for boons. By this time it was quite clear to him that her demand was not ordinary, otherwise she could have simply come to him and asked for boons of her desire. But she had to hatch such a big plot for this; he got suspicious that her demand would be unjust and unsuitable. Dashratha felt that even if he beat his brow against the wall, he would not be able to peep through Kaikeyi's mind. His whole being was now unsafe. He was waiting for explosion in the form of Kaikeyi's boons. "Then listen to me, Maharaja!" said Kaikeyi in her intense and steady voice. "I come to my first boon. I want that patient and noble-minded Shri Rama should be exiled from the kingdom for fourteen years. He should be wearing only bark clothes and deer skin. My second boon is that Bharata should be Ayodhya's king without any impediment. Both the boons must immediately be fulfilled."

Dashratha felt as if two fire-branded arrows had been shot at him. One got stuck in his chest and the other in his throat. His breath and heart-beats stopped functioning. He murmured something, "Hey Rama!" And then he fell down on the ground like a large tree that had been chopped off.

* * *